THE ORIGINS OF THE CHANGOS

Dumitru Mărtinaş

THE ORIGINS OF THE CHANGOS

Edited by Vasile M. Ungureanu

The Center for Romanian Studies
Las Vegas ◊ Oxford ◊ Palm Beach

Published in the United States of America by

Histria Books, a division of Histria LLC

7181 N. Hualapai Way

Las Vegas, NV 89166 USA

HistriaBooks.com

The Center for Romanian Studies is an imprint of Histria Books. Titles published under the imprints of Histria Books are distributed worldwide.

Library of Congress Control Number: 2020939980

ISBN 978-973-98391-4-3 (Hardcover)
ISBN 978-1-59211-079-7 (Softbound)

Table of Contents

Introduction

No matter how precise a scholar's field of specialization may be, through his creative work, he walks the thorny path of ideas. However, unlike the fakir who arrives alone on the other side of the pit full of hot embers, the scholar creates a solid path so that others who follow him may have safe passage and venture on new thorny paths themselves.

Dumitru Mărtinaş took his place in the history of culture through his studies in which he expressed his desire to make us understand once again that all persons are part of the wonderful and grand concert of peoples. He understood that, like any individual, he was at the same time both an agent and a witness to human unity and solidarity, and this is how he expressed himself insistently in his writings. His work, completed by editors with careful accuracy so as not alter in any way its content and shape, was the result of years of scholarship. This synthesis of his work appears now, for the first time, in English. This book is his answer to the primordial question: Who am I? Persevering in this quest, he discovered himself in relation to his fellow human beings, for in seeking the origins of the Changos he discovered his own origins, as he too belonged to this group of people: alike or different, that is *stem* or *hybrid,* corresponding in the Magyar language to *törzs vagy csángó.*

In the Romanian lands, Slavic influence led to Romanian Catholics being looked upon as hybrids, similar, on a different level, to the Szecklers (Magyars) who, coming from Transylvania to Moldavia, accepted to live within the Romanian environment on the other side of the Carpathians. Catholics (even indigenous ones) became allogenic, as the center of their religion was outside the Romanian Principalities, giving foreign powers a pretext to intervene for religious reasons and to establish a protectorate.

It is well-known that, in many parts of Romania, there is a lexical identity between the words *German* and *mechanic,* a kind of technical hybridization of the Romanians with the Germans. To claim the Changos as Magyars – by applying a word meaning *hybrid*, according to a simple religious criterion – Catholicism – would be as if Germany would claim the Germans in Romania according to a professional criterion – that of mechanic. This is what Dumitru Mărtinaş demonstrates in this remarkable book, the first on the subject written by a member of this population.

In the early nineteenth century, Alexandru Cosma from Chiuruş, near Târgu Secuiesc – known by the Magyar name of Körösi Csoma Sándor, March 1784-11 April 1842) – traveled from Wallachia (1819) to Tibet, to discover, through comparative linguistic studies, the place of origin and the ancientness of the Magyar people. His thesis, maintaining that the Magyar language derived from the Sanskrit language, considered to be the matrix of languages on Earth, was invalidated long ago. The fervent disputes about priority, which gradually arose as a result of extreme nationalism, did not cease afterwards, but, on the contrary, increased in intensity.

In Moldavia, during the same period, the Catholic bishop Ioan Filip Paroni (2 August 1818-19 June 1825) tried to revoke the Turkish firman that interdicted his residence in Iaşi by accepting an Austrian protectorate, which was not recognized by the Porte. His relations with the consul Iosif Raab, the Hapsburg representative in Iaşi, led to a serious conflict with the state authorities and with Metropolitan Veniamin Costache, and because of his adversity with the superiors at the Congregation of Fide Propaganda, with the leadership of the Conventual-Franciscan Order, and with the local missionaries, he had to leave Moldavia. To build a defense for himself, under the pretext of the necessity of protection for the Catholics on the other side of the Carpathians, he associated himself with the Magyar missionaries whose number he increased through a convention with the Franciscan superior in Cluj, concluded immediately after his mandate (25 July 1825) and subsequently ratified after much insistence (8 April 1826). This measure served to prolong the Austrian protectorate in Moldavia.

The result was that the offensive of the Magyar missionaries against the Italian missionaries became stronger, and the Orthodox-Catholic conflict was aggravated by proselytism and a policy of deliberate Magyarization of the Romanian population (Catholic or non-Catholic, of Romanian or Magyar language.). This situation became known to the Vatican through a long series of interventions regarding Moldavia: signals of religious and human alarm, some of which, as we find in archives, are true social panoramas: the Apostolic Visitor Giuseppe Tomassi, sent to make investigations in Moldavia – 10 December 1858 (the Archives of the Congregation of Fide Propaganda, SC, Moldavia, volume II, ff. 805r-850v), Bishop Antoine Joseph Plyum – 9 October 1868 (Id., SC, Valachia, volume 14, ff. 484r-485r and onward), and Bishop Nicolo Camilli – 8 August 1883 (Id., Sc., Moldavia, volume 13, fo. 150+v and onward). Their reports reflect, as a common denominator, the tendency of the Magyar missionaries to denationalize the Romanians. The prelates mentioned above wrote that, in Moldavia, if all the Hungarians spoke Romanian, not all the Romanians spoke Hungarian, and while none of the Italian missionaries were Romanianizing the Magyars, the Magyar missionaries were doing their best to Magyarize the Romanians, aiming at territorial expansion over Moldavia and Wallachia.

The contemporary epoch, with the possibility of scholarly analysis through various means of investigation, has offered interdisciplinary works showing that the decreed "Changoization" has resulted from the reality that all Changos are Catholics. The bibliography on this problem has been enriched through a recent book by Kós Károly, Szentimrei Judit, and Dr. Nagy Jenö, benefiting mostly by illustrations and an excellent editorial technique, the iconography exceeding or contradicting in some chapters the text. The important thing is that the authors bring evidence of Romanian popular art having been assimilated for a long time and with great power even in villages where the Catholics declare themselves to be of Szeckler (Magyar) origin, in a unity which is an inherent part of Moldavian art (of course we are not talking of the exaggerations according to which the potter's wheel, the scissors, the spindle shuttle, and so on were "achievements" of Chango culture and civilization, introduced into the Romanian patrimony). But even with its imprecisions, this book is a positive event in the study of Romanian ethnography, being far less biased than older works. The reader will understand how far it is from the epoch in which the instigators, professional or dilettantes, tried to incite spirits with the "amiableness" of the protectorate, a protectorate which was never solicited by those whom the "protectors" called "hybrids" (the euphemistic term proposed by us does not correspond to the pejorative one in the Magyar language – csángó).

As the present volume attests, there is a large bibliography with tendentious titles dealing with this problem, and this is why Dumitru Mărtinaş elucidates, in a scholarly manner, the ethnic identity of himself and his people. In our times, their specific ethnic and spiritual features found their expression in the monumentality of certain public edifices which use as their prototype a peasant from Sasca (in the county of Suceava) – Ieremia Valahul – who was beatified by Pope John Paul II as "the first Romanian promoted to the dignity of Rome's altars." His integration into the history of Romanian Catholicism proves that the problem has been neglected or not understood by scholars and that it imposes scientific objectivity. Future scholars will continue the work begun by Dumitru Mărtinaş and will enrich scholarship through their exploration of Romanian culture.

The book is edited by Vasile M. Ungureanu, a philologist in Cluj, himself a Chango from Sagna (in the county of Neamţ), who is the author of the editor's notes that enhance the author's original text. Ion Coja coedited the original Romanian text, together with Vasile Ungureanu. The reader will find in the text of this book and in the notes the viewpoints of two Changos, Dumitru Mărtinaş and Vasile M. Ungureanu, regarding their origins and ethnic allegiance. Their conclusions are drawn from the tradition in which they were born and grew up, as well as the results of years of historical and linguistic research that bore out the popular tradition of their Romanian origin.

Ion Dumitru-Snagov

Author's Preface

The history of research on the Changos is full of long, adventurous, and very often futile searches. This problem has held the attention of scholars because of their Magyar dialect, which can still be heard in a few villages in Moldavia. This gave rise to a long controversy centered around the strange non-Magyar phonetic system of this dialect, a controversy that has not as yet ceased. Although investigations of the Changos are old and often required an arduous scholarly effort, to date, they have not led to satisfactory results. The efforts of historians proved useless when faced with the complexity and obscurity, apparently unsolvable, of this historical-linguistic phenomenon. In Gustav Weigand's opinion, the presence of this population on the territory of Romania represents a historical enigma, *ein Rätsel*. A more recent scholar who studied this problem, Géza Bakó, said, in 1962, that the problem in itself was still unsolved at that time. Although it is not known how and from where they appeared, the ancestors of unknown origin of the Changos were supposedly assimilated by the Magyars long ago, in circumstances which remain obscure, and then, in a more recent epoch, it is assumed that they were denationalized in their great majority by the Moldavian Romanians. What was, however, the origin of the primitive Changos? Who were their ancestors? Where was their initial land situated? What was their original language? What is the significance behind their strange name, *Changos*? All these represent still unsolved problems for researchers.

In 1766, the Szeckler missionary Petru Zöld discovered that the Changos he visited were bilingual: *Omnes linguam moldavicam sive valachicam aeque ac hungaricam et callent, et loquuntur* ("All of them know and speak equally well both Romanian and Hungarian"). For the deciphering of the uncertain past of a bilingual population, a thorough study of both languages spoken by that population is necessary. The scholar today finds himself surprised by the fact that, up to now, all scholarly research has avoided the study of the Romanian Chango dialect, linguists being concerned exclusively with the problems of their Hungarian dialect. Involuntarily, the reader asks himself: why did scholars in the past avoid researching the Romanian dialect spoken by the majority of this population, considering such research useless and inconclusive? Why has the Romanian linguistic aspect of the problem been looked upon as non-existent, avoided, ignored, and thrust into semi-darkness by scholars?

It seems that the "enigmatic" Changos in Moldavia came here in roundabout ways from a lesser-known epoch of Romanian history. The abolishing of their past being impossible, scholars tried to adjust it. In this long and toilsome effort of "correction", an element of great scientific importance was forgotten: their Romanian dialect. It was thought that by passing over the original language of the population in silence and by substituting it with a foreign language, which it never acquired correctly, its historical past could be forgotten, and its assimilation by the Hungarian population would be ensured. This experience failed, as the Changos never forgot their native language. The history of this problem will be discussed in the pages of this book.

Inverting the procedure used up to now in the research of this phenomenon, the present study concentrates first of all, on the Romanian dialect of the Changos, which differs significantly from that of the Romanians living in Moldavia.

The thorough study of this important linguistic and historical document opens for scholars a whole different perspective on the historical past of this population from that which has been espoused by linguists and historians up to now. The unveiling of this past, which was considered for a long time an enigma, is of great interest for Romanian history, because the origins of the Chango population should not be sought in the nebulous epoch of the migration of peoples, as some authors have tried to do in the past, but it is the result of more recent historical processes, which took place some time ago in the open, but around which, over time, the legend of an enigma has been created.

By pointing out the old problem of the Szecklerization of the Romanians and emphasizing the inherent link between this historical process and the appearance of the Changos in Transylvania, we do not intend to reopen a thorny problem, which we can regret, but which cannot be reversed, and which, at the same time, cannot be forgotten or ignored. We only want to offer to scholars and to the public the key to understanding the "enigma" of the Changos, a problem long considered to be indecipherable, which past investigations failed to elucidate, *not* because the phenomenon was indecipherable in itself, but because, in their great majority, those who studied it did not, for various reasons, approach the problem in the proper scholarly manner.

The process of Szecklerization of numerous Romanian villages in southeastern Transylvania belongs to times buried forever by historical evolution. Today, respect for the language, culture, and individuality of any people is part of the respect and appreciation we give to the cultural values of all humankind. In this spirit, we sought the origins of the Changos in Moldavia so that they may, as is their right, be considered what they are and not something else.

Dumitru Mărtinaş

Part I
Historical Aspects

Chapter 1

An Old Historical Controversy: The Origins of the Changos

Before dealing with the problem of the Romanian dialect of the Changos,[1] it is necessary to discuss the historical and geographical aspects of the problem of the origins of the Changos and to make certain distinctions known. These are intended to facilitate the understanding of the linguistic facts and to eliminate, from the beginning, a series of confusions which have contributed a great deal to misleading scholars in the past and to creating the almost inextricable intricacy of the problem.

From a geographical point of view, the village population in Moldavia, known under the popular name of *Hungarians* and in

---

[1] (Editor's Note) The author uses the name *Changos* (*ceangăi*) because it is frequent in the writings concerning the Catholic population in Moldavia. The term was adopted by the Romanians from Hungarian publications, and, just like the popular name of *Hungarians*, it is not used by those who are called this way, who consider themselves *Catholic Romanians*. "All the Catholics in Moldavia perceive the name Chango as a nickname given to them by foreigners. The word *Chango* is not of Romanian origin; it is Hungarian. Therefore they perceive the Hungarians as foreigners." (Dumitru Mărtinaş, *Caietul Alfa,* I, p. 138). See also the observation of a geographer: "…and they do not like it when you call them Hungarians or Changos; they say they are Catholic Romanians" (Victor Tufescu, "O regiune de vie circulaţie: 'poarta Târgului-Frumos,'" in *Buletinul Societăţii Regale Române de Geografie,* LIX, 1940, p. 372). See notes 5, 24, and 69, as well as the comment by the author on page 37.

scholarly circles under the name of *Changos,* is not a homogeneous population and does not live in a precise area. It is dispersed among the mass of native Moldavians living in the middle basin of the Siret River, from Paşcani, in the north, to where the Trotuş and Siret rivers meet, as well as to the east, in the county of Iaşi, and to the west, in the county of Neamţ.

From the point of view of their origins, the Changos can be divided into two different ethnic categories:

a) First, the great majority of the Changos concentrated in the region of the cities of Roman (the northern group) and Bacău (the southern group), about whom it is known for certain that they are not Szecklers;[2] they wear Romanian national costumes, most of them speak Romanian in a specific Transylvanian dialect and live according to Romanian ways and customs. Given the language they speak, their traditions, and their ethnographic heritage, this is a population of Transylvanian Romanians, as will be demonstrated later on.

b) Second, in terms of numerical importance, there is a group of Changos of Szeckler origin (around 25,000 people), the great majority living in the valleys of the Trotuş and Tazlău rivers, and a few in the Siret valley, their native dialect being very close to the Szeckler one, having Szeckler customs, and their way of life being similar to that of the Szecklers. Today, most of them are bilingual, speaking the Moldavian dialect of Romanian fluently as well. They live in approximately 30 localities, mixed with Romanian Moldavians.

These two populations, although they are known under the same generic name of *Hungarians* or *Changos,* in reality, are two distinct

---

[2]The fact is emphasized by the Magyar historian Mikecs László, *Csángók* (*The Changos*), Budapest, 1941, p. 13 (Editor's Note: A century earlier, after a trip to Moldavia, Elek Gegö wrote the following: "...all those... who maintain with certainty that the Hungarian settlements in Moldavia are of Szeckler origin are wrong," *A moldavi magyar telepekröl,* p. 68).

peoples, different through their language and ethnicity, through their customs and consciousness. The Szecklers do not consider themselves Changos, and the Changos do not consider themselves Szecklers. This is a well-established fact, recognized by scholars such as Nicolae Iorga, Radu Rosetti, Gustav Weigand, and Laszlo Mikecs. In this sense, we specify that only the Changos in the first category use the sibilant pronunciation /s/ instead of /sh/ and /z/ instead of /zh/, while the others do not. The mistaken identification of these two populations as belonging to the ethnic group has generated numerous errors in scholarship and much confusion.

***

It is well known that scholarship in general, both Hungarian and Romanian, considers the Changos to be a population of non-Romanian origin, usually Magyar. On the other hand, the Changos do not consider themselves Magyars, but *Catholics* or *Romanian Catholics*, thus preserving the tradition recorded by Dimitrie Cantemir about the Moldavian Catholics of his time, who declared themselves Catholics, both by nation, as well as by religion: *tum natione, tum religione, ut se vocant Catholici.*[3]

Unfortunately, for two centuries after the recording of this tradition, no Romanian scholar dealt specifically with the problem of the Catholic population in Moldavia, considering it to be a question of interest mainly to Hungarian researchers. Thus, those who studied the problem ignored systematically the very approach from which they could have solved the "enigma", whose approach as a Hungarian problem did not lead to any conclusive results.

---

[3]Dimitrie Cantemir, *Descrierea Moldovei*, Bucureşti, 1973, p. 2.

The appearance of the first Romanian studies dedicated to the Chango phenomenon marks the beginning of the ultimate resolution of this controversial problem. The hypothesis regarding the Romanian origin of the Changos explains both the linguistic evidence and the historical facts related to the problem. The most important Romanian works on the subject were written by Iosif Petru M. Pal[4] and Petru Râmneanțu.[5] The valuable suggestion made by Nicolae Iorga regarding the mystery hidden in the old Transylvanian costume, which led him to the conclusion that "they are far from being as foreign as one might presume,"[6] must also be mentioned.

From a social and political point of view, the problem of this population was pointed out to the Romanians already in the mid-nineteenth century, at the Ad-Hoc Divan in Moldavia in 1857, by Mihail Kogălniceanu, who had words of generous political and human understanding, supporting civil rights for the Changos.[7] When some of

---

[4]Iosif Petru M. Pal, *Originea catolicilor din Moldova și Franciscanii, păstorii lor de veacuri,* Săbăoani-Roman, 1942, 264 pp.

[5]Petru Râmneanțu, *Die Abstrammung der Tschangos,* Sibiu, 1944, 64 pp.; *Problema iradierii românilor din Transilvania în principatele romăne,* Cluj, 1946, 163 pp.

[6]Nicolae Iorga, *România cum era până la 1918. II Moldova și Dobrogea,* București, 1940, p.181. (Editor's Note: The characterization dates from 1907, when Nicolae Iorga made a trip by carriage from Roman to Șcheia, along the Siret valley. The intuition of the historian is also strengthened by these observations: "Catholic student in Iași, sons of foreigners, but born in Romania, and a few sons of Romanian peasants of the Latin religion" (in reality the sons of Romanian peasants were the most numerous, n.n.); he dedicated a volume to Bishop Camili ("Talente necunoscute," in *Floarea darurilor,* I, 1907, nr. 2, p. 117); also: "the Hungarian mountain peasants call themselves Romanians"' (*Oameni cari au fost,* II, București, 1935, p. 192).

[7](Editor's Note) Kogălniceanu had included the rights of the Catholic Romanians also in *Dorințele* partied *naționale din Moldova* (points 25 and 26). Point 25 states: "Over 50,000 Romanians are Catholics. Until now, the government has not concerned itself at all with their moral and religious education. Their clergy is foreign and is not supported by the state. It is, therefore, necessary that these sons of the country benefit from public advantages as well" (see Mihail Kogălniceanu, *Dorințele partide*

the deputies in the assembly argued that the catholic villagers should be denied political rights,[8] Mihail Kogălniceanu, supported by Costache Negri, defended with conviction their legitimate rights, which they had earned by living and working side by side with the Orthodox villagers. At the meeting of 12 November 1857, the great politician made the following judicious considerations: "Let me show you now what kind of future awaits us if the proposal is rejected: thousands of inhabitants will thus be declared without rights, although they take part in all the obligations, pay taxes, perform military service, and share in all the hardships of the country. Every one of these inhabitants, declared foreigners in their own country, would be entitled to say the same thing that, at the first elections, a Catholic inhabitant from Săbăoani, elected deputy for the county of Roman, replied to the subprefect, who would not recognize him as deputy because he was a Catholic: 'Why, sir, if all the villages elected me to defend their rights in the Great Assembly, although I am a Catholic, can I not be a deputy? But when you collect our taxes, when we give you our sons to serve in the army, when we do statute labor for you, why are we not Catholics then, but are regarded as Orthodox believers? Sir, if we cannot be deputies because we are Catholics, then

---

naționale din Moldova, third edition, published by Petre V. Haneş, Bucureşti, f.a., pp. 30-31). For information about the interest of Kogălniceanu in the Catholics of Moldavia, see Alexandru Zub, "Preocupări de istorie eclesiastică la M. Kogălniceanu," in *Mitropolia Moldovei şi Sucevei*, XLIX, 1973, nr. 3-4, martie-aprilie, p. 232, and V. Palade, "Principii de drept biscricesc în opera lui Mihail Kogălniceanu," *ibidem*, LI, 1975, nr. 3-4, martie-aprilie, pp. 299-300.

[8](Editor's Note) Especially Gheorghieş Sturdza, the representative of the great landowner in the region of Roman, who justified his attitude stating that he was a Romanian. Criticizing false patriotism, Kogălniceanu's answer was prompt: "...I am also a Romanian, and more than he is. Mine is an old Romanian family; I am a freeholder, a native of Cogălnic.... But the question is not who is more or less Romanian..., the question is who defends a just idea" (see Dimitre A. Sturdza and C. Colescu-Vartic, *Acte şi documente relative la renascerea României*, VI/I, p. 229).

let us be Catholics when we pay our taxes and do all our labors.'[9] Let us think seriously, gentlemen, about what we are doing. By rejecting the proposal, it is not only that we do not give, but we actually take away rights that have been held for hundreds of years by natives like

---

[9](Editor's Note) This deputy for the county of Roman was Ianuş Robu (see also the speech from 20 January 1865, in Mihail Kogălniceanu, *Opere*, IV. *Oratorie*, II/I, Bucureşti, 1977, p. 58). The injustice was rectified during the elections on 24 and 25 November 1864, when he was elected deputy in the Elective Assembly of Romania (see *Dezbaterile Adunării Elective a României*, 1865, nr. 1, p. 2). The historian Lajos Demeny has recently tackled the problem of the political rights of the Catholic population in Moldavia in the Ad-hoc Divan in two articles ("Bonyodalmak egy képviseliválasztás korul. (I) Csángok az egyes, lés korában" – "Avatars around a Deputy Election (I). The Changos in the Period of the Union," in *A hét*, XIII, 1982, no. 19, 7 May, p. 8, and "Kogălniceanu a moldvai Országgy, lésben egyenli jogokat követel a csángóknak" – "Kogălniceanu Asks for Equal Rights for the Changos in the Moldavian Divan," *ibidem*, no. 20, 14 May, p. 8), to which we specify: 1) the name of the deputy was Ianuş (pronounced Ianus) Robu, not "Rab János," as the author writes; 2) Kogălniceanu did not ask equal rights for the "Changos", but for the Catholic inhabitants who, "in their great majority," were "of true Romanian origin" (see Mihail Kogălniceanu, *Opere* III, *Oratorie*. I/I, Bucureşti, 1983, p. 207), "so we can be this way one single nation: the Romanian nation" and "have and defend one single country: beautiful Romania!" (Dimitrie A. Sturza and C. Colescu-Vartie, *op. cit.*, p. 238).

One of the grandsons of deputy Robu was Mihai Robu (1884, Săbăoani-1944, Beius, later reburied in Iaşi), the first Romanian bishop of the Catholic diocese in Iaşi. "Born and raised in Romania, having a traditional peasant name from this region, knowing the needs of the population… and the interests of the Romanian state to which he must feel tied with his whole being" (Nicolae Iorga), Bishop Robu, in the time of whom the diocese knew a period of spiritual and national flourishing, fully confirmed through his activity the statement he made in the year of his investment: "I will never forget that I am a son of the Romanian people and I will work with all my might for its flourishing" (see *Neamul românesc*, XX, 1925, 26 septembrie, p. 1, and nr. 226, 9 octombrie, p. 2). About him, see Iosif E. Naghiu, "Episcopul Mihai Robu," in *Universul*, LXI, 1944, nr. 289, 25 octombrie, p. 3.

Ioan Robu (originally from Traian, in the commune of Săbăoani) is part of the same illustrious family; he is presently apostolic administrator of the Catholic Archdiocese in Bucharest, sanctioned bishop in Rome on 8 December 1984, his mission being to continue, on a larger scale, the work of his predecessor in Iaşi.

the Catholic freeholders in the regions of Bacău and Iaşi. They have always considered themselves natives, enjoying all civic and political rights."[10]

Costache Negri declared, on the same occasion: "As for the Catholic natives, there is not much to talk about; there are 50 or 60 thousand of them, who, together with us, for centuries, in all our moments of trial and tribulation, have endured all the sufferings that the Lord our God wished to admonish us with, to bring us on the path of wisdom and justice that we need today... I am going to conclude with a great precept of our holy and gracious Christian religion: treat others as you would want them to treat you. We ask for rights; we must give rights."[11]

As a result of the arguments put forth by these Romanian leaders, the political rights of the Catholic inhabitants of Moldavia were subsequently recognized. Nevertheless, Romanian public opinion and Romanian scholars remained misinformed or little interested in them, adhering to the conclusions of certain Magyar scholars, which they

---

[10]Dimitrie A. Sturdza and C. Colescu-Varti, *Acte şi documente relative la* renascerea *Românei,* vol. VI, part I. *Divanul Ad-hoc al Moldovei din 1857,* Bucuresci, pp. 232-233, 237-238 (Editor's Note: Other significant passages on pp. 238-242. The Discourse is reproduced in Mihail Kogălniceanu, *op. cit.,* pp. 50-62). Some aspects in the discourse of Kogălniceanu are found in the appeal of Bishop Antonio de Stefano, *apostolic locum tenens* of Moldavia, from March 1857, addressed to the European Commission for the Reorganization of the Romanian Principalities. Of Italian origin, an ecclesiastical writer of Romanian language, who knew the realities of Moldavia very well, he used in this document the term *les Catholiques Roumains* (he also had printed in 1848, in Braşov, a catechism for "Dacian-Roman-Catholics"). He participated as a guest at the opening of the Ad-hoc Divan and collaborated closely with the Unionist Party, opposing the maneuvers of the Austrian consular agent Gödel, a supporter of the anti-unionists, and fighting for the recognizing of the political rights of the Catholic Romanians in Moldavia. About his activity, see I, Dumitru-Snagov, *Le Saint-Siège et la Roumaine moderne 1850-1866,* Rome, 1982, pp. 46-56.

[11]*Ibidem,* p. 24.

accepted without critical analysis, especially considering the linguistic evidence on which these conclusions were based. This is why, even today, students of philology are taught about the Magyar origin of these Catholic inhabitants, a conclusion which, not long ago, even the state believed, treating them as an ethnic Magyar minority, with all the legal provisions. As a result, the Romanian state created schools for the Changos with Magyar as the language of instruction and with a syllabus geared toward Magyar culture.[12] However, the Changos refused to attend these schools and protested that denationalization was being imposed upon them, asking for Romanian schools instead. The tradition of their Romanian origins and the common sense of unity proved stronger than any outside influences. But neither public opinion nor the authorities, nor the press, especially the foreign press, succeeded in understanding the real significance of what was, at that time, around 1950, called "the absurd gesture" of this population. In fact, the gesture was not absurd, as we will demonstrate later, but was a logical action, a consequence of a long and difficult history largely unknown to Romanian public opinion.[13]

On the occasion of an interesting controversy around the question of language and dialect, Romulus Todoran, a linguist in Cluj, dealt in short with the "Chango dialect," "spoken by the largest group of Magyar population in Moldavia," a branch of the Magyar language, with an isolated existence and a peculiar development within the Hungarian language, which, however, disappears gradually through its mixture with the Romanian language.[14]

---

[12]Cf. *Introducere in lingvistică,* 2nd edition, Bucureşti, 1965, p. 281 (Editor's Note: The third edition (Bucureşti, 1972) does not include any mention of the Changos).

[13]See also *infra,* pp. 50,130.

[14]Romulus Todoran, "Cu privire la o problemă de lingvistică in discuţie: limbă şi dialect," in *Cercetări de lingvistică,* I, 1956, pp. 97-98 (Editor's Note: See also D. Marcea: "The influence of the Romanian language on the dialect of the Changos in

Statements of this kind were the result of the lack of sufficient information in this field, which explains, but does not justify, the error in which Romanian linguistics persists.

If Magyar historians and linguists paid proper attention, and with good reasons, to the Hungarian dialect spoken by a few thousand Changos who were more profoundly affected by the process of Szecklerization, it is necessary, in the interest of scholarship, that equal attention be paid to the Romanian Transylvanian dialect spoken until recently by the great majority of the Changos (around 200,000), and still spoken today by many of them, especially women and old people, mainly from the villages of the northern group. The study of this dialect brings forth very interesting and edifying linguistic and historical facts regarding the origin and the historical past of this population. If it is indisputable that linguistic analysis can be regarded as a valuable historical tool, previous conceptions about the Changos will have to be reconsidered in this light.

As far as the ethnic origin of the Changos is concerned, scholars in the past, almost all of them Hungarian, disseminated a series of hypothesis and legends, which later on proved to be heavily influenced by the Romanticism and Nationalism characteristics of the epoch. Thus, the Magyar historian Gegö Elek, sent in 1837 by the Magyar Society of Sciences to visit and study the Changos in Moldavia, found so many non-Magyar elements in their language, costume, appearance, customs, and way of life that, overlooking visible Romanian ethnographic characteristics, he drew the conclusion that they were of Cuman origin, although no historical, linguistic, or ethnographic

---

Moldavia is very strong. They have been living, since the Middle Ages, in the middle of a compact mass of Romanians, their number is small, and they are all bilingual" (*Probleme ale structurii şi evoluţiei limbii române*, Bucureşti, 1982, pp. 95-96). It is obvious that, unlike others, the author considers only the bilingual minority of the Chango population).

evidence supported such conclusions.[15] Knowing that the characteristics he observed were not Magyar, and failing to consider that they could be Romanian, the historian took refuge in the Cuman hypothesis, admitting, indirectly, the non-Magyar character of this population.

Later on, Gustav Weigand also adopted the hypothesis concerning their Cuman origin on the basis of the sibilant pronunciation, a phenomenon characteristic of the phonetic traditions which, he assumed, without any proof, were belated reflex of the Cuman language.[16] The German linguistic also noticed a series of incontestable Romanian aspects among the Changos, but, like some Magyar authors, he considered that these resulted from a recent and strong Romanian influence among the Magyarized Cumans.[17]

The Magyar historian Karácsonyi János assumed, without plausible evidence, that they were the descendants of a group of Cabars, an Asian population that was in the pay of the Magyars during the period in which they occupied Pannonia, although no linguistic or

---

[15]Gegö Elek, *A moldvai magyar telepekröl (About the Hungarian Settlements in Moldavia)*, Budán, 1838, pp. 62-68 (Editor's Note: The work was presented at large by the geographer Ioan Rusu, "Insemnări asupra călătoriei P (ărintelui) A. Gegö in Moldova," in *Foaie pentru minte, inimă şi literatura*, II, 1839, nr. 43-46; reproduced in *Societatea Geografică Română. Buletin*, III, 1892, pp. 56-73. The author uses the word *Hăngăi* for *Ceangăi*/Changos).

[16]Gustav Weigand, "Der Ursprung der s-Gemeinden," in *Neunter Jahresbericht des Institutes fur Rumanische Sprache (Rumanisches Seminar) zu Leipzig*, 1902, p. 137.

[17](Editor's Note) See also the study "Die Dialekte der Moldau und Dobrudscha," in *Neunter Jahresbericht...*, pp. 138-236. Georges D. Cioriceanu maintains a Cuman-Romanian symbiosis for the Changos who speak Hungarian: "Les Ciangai, parlant le hongrois, de confession catholique et s'habillant à la roumaine, ne sont, en majorité, que des Coumans et des Roumains melanges. Ils sont venus de Transylvanie" (*La Roumanie économique et ses rapports avec l'étranger de 1860 à 1915*, Paris, 1928, p. 64, note 2).

ethnographic connection can be established between the Cabars and the Changos.[18]

Other historians considered a possible Pecheneg origin of the Changos. Even Nicolae Iorga, during a conference in 1918, put forward the hypothesis that they could be descendants of an ancient Turkish population, established in Moldavia before the appearance of the Magyars in Europe, which allegedly gave the names to certain mountains in the Eastern Carpathians (Rarău, Ceahlău).[19] This hypothesis could not be confirmed by linguistic studies either.

The hypothesis of the Cuman origin of the Changos was widely accepted for a time. All the unknown aspects of this problem, including the sibilant pronunciation, were attributed to a presumed Cuman origin. In other words, an unknown factor (the origin of the Changos) was explained through another unknown factor (the origin of the sibilant pronunciation). And because, for a time, some historians considered the Cumans as being a people related to the Huns, there was even the assumption of their Hunish origin.[20]

---

[18]Karácsonyi János, *A moldvai csángók credete* (*The Origin of the Changos in Moldavia*), Budapest, 1914, p. 18; apud Veress Endre, *A moldvai csángók származása ès neve* (*The Origin and the Name of the Changos in Moldavia*), Cluj, 1934, p. 22. (Editor's Note: Sandor N. Szilágyi comes with a new opinion, namely the Cabar-Cazar origin of the Changos, "Amit még nem mondtak el a csángó névril" – "What Has Not Yet Been Said about the Name of Chango," in A hét.

[19]Nicolae Iorga, "Considerații noi asupra rostului secuilor," in *Revista istorică*, XXV, 1939, nr. 4-6, aprilie-iunie, p. 141 (Editor's Note: Nicolae Iorga considered it "a new point of view," formulating it as follows: "...it is an old Turkish population, that was able to give names to a few of the summits of the Carpathians" and that, "remaining independent, organized itself together with the Romanians in these 'Romance' forms, to which the political creations of popular character were added").

[20]Petru Râmneanțu, *Die Abstammung der Tschangos*, p. 11 (Editor's Note: Certainly, it is more a reflex of the presumed Hun origin of the Szecklers, maintained by the Hungarian chroniclers).

According to other authors, the Changos are the descendants of a group of Magyars from Atelkuz, who, not wanting to go on to Pannonia, preferred to settle on the valleys of the Siret, Moldova, and Bistriţa rivers.[21]

While Magyar scholars attributed all sorts of ethno-historical antecedents to the Changos, without being able to decide on any one in particular, Romanian historians in the past (A.D. Xenopol, D. Onciul, Radu Rosetti, and so on) agreed on the fact that the Changos represented a population of Magyar origin.[22] Their Catholicism in particular, and the Hungarian dialect of a small part of them, seemed to them to be proof of their Magyar origin.

The religious criterion did not prove sufficient either to resolve the controversial problem of the ethnic origin of the Changos. The first to realize this were Magyar linguists. Unlike historians, they adopted

---

[21]Györffi István, *A moldvai csángók* (*The Changos in Moldavia*), Budapest, 1917. (Editor's Note: I have not seen the quoted work. However, in *Moldva* (Budapest, 1916), the same author sees in the Changos a mixture of different kinds of Hungarians and foreigners, with sibilant pronunciation adopted from the Cumans, which they still preserved when they were completely Romanianized (p. 20). About the Szecklers on the Trotuş he says that they are not one and the same as the Changos and they despise each other (p. 23). We mention that Romanian scholars have also talked about the Dacian origin of the Changos, as vestiges of the Kaukoens tribe, see M. Gârniţeanu, "Catolicii ciangăi din Moldova sunt daci. Daci care trăiesc şi azi" – "The Catholic Changos in Moldavia are Dacians. Dacian Who Still Live Today," in Lumina Creştinului, XXX, 1944, februarie, cover 3-4; reproduced from Moldova, III, 1944, 26 Januarie, p. 2).

[22](Editor's Note) Ilie Minea was working however on a study about their Romanian origin (see Emil Diaconescu, "Opera ştiinţifică a profesorului Ilie Minea" – "The Scientific Work of Professor Ilie Minea," in Studii şi cercetări istorice, Iaşi, XVIII, 1943, p. 23). Manuscript about the Catholic in Moldavia remained from George Pascu, a linguist and literary historian (see Iosif E. Naghiu) and from Petru Cancel (1890-1947), a Slavicist, himself of Chango origin. (see Radu-Ştefan Ciobanu, "Puncte de vedere asupra ceangăilor," – "Opinions on the Origin of the Changos," in Flacăra, XXXI, 1982, nr. 1, 7 Januarie, p. 10).

another research criterion, the linguistic one. These linguists were, with good reason, intrigued and confused by the fact that the phonetic system of the Chango Hungarian dialect was so alien to the phonological tradition of the Magyar language, so that for them it was obvious that the ancestors of the Changos were not Magyars, but belonged to another basis of articulation, to another phonological tradition, to another language, to another ethnic origin.[23]

The ethnicity of their ancestors remained, however, an unsolved problem. These scholars were concerned with finding out what was the language of the proto-Changos and where their initial native land was situated. To shed light on this problem, Magyar scholars undertook ample investigations in different geographic regions, from the western border with Austria to the far lands of Asia, but they could not recover any traces of the Changos anywhere. Neither the language, nor the native land, nor the origin of their ancestors could be identified. Not even the family of languages to which that primitive language might have belonged could be determined, or if it is still spoken somewhere or died out without a trace in the chaotic confusion of the migration of peoples. Generations of scientists, historians, and linguists tried, without success, to solve this problem. In 1941, Domokos Pál Péter expressed his bewilderment this way: "It is hard to find an answer to the questions: who are the Changos in Moldavia? When did they settle on the territories they are living on today? Who Christianized them in the Catholic religion and when? Who taught them to speak Hungarian?"[24]

---

[23]For details regarding this research, see Szabó T. Attila, "A moldvai csángó nyelvjáráskutatás története" ("The History of Research on the Dialect of the Changos in Moldavia"), in *Magyar nyelvjárások*, Budapest, V, 1959, pp. 3-41.

[24]Domokos Pál Peter, *A moldvai magyarság* (*The Hungarians in Moldavia*), Cluj, 1941, p. 238.

While the historical origins of the Changos remained a mystery to this author, he nevertheless asserted that the Changos belong, without any doubt, to the Magyar nation, as they speak or once speak Hungarian, and that their Romanian language of today was borrowed from the Moldavians in a recent epoch and is the result of denationalization. This statement remains unfounded, as long as their Romanian language is not taken into consideration, and without it, the "enigma" of the phenomenon cannot be solved.

An interesting moment in the history of this controversy came when the Romanian biologist Petru Râmneanțu, using a new method of investigation, analyzing blood groups, established that the Changos have the same biological index as the Romanians and that their origin is Romanian.[25] Certain foreign political circles did not agree with this argument, and following powerful diplomatic pressure from Baron Manfred von Killinger, Nazi Germany's ambassador to Bucharest, the book was withdrawn from circulation.

More recently, again taking up research on the problem of the origins of the Changos, Géza Bakó reached the conclusion that the sibilant pronunciation was, in times past, part of a territorial Magyar dialect in the region of the rivers Rába and Repce, close to the border with Austria. The ancestors of the Changos supposedly belonged to this group of Magyars, who lived in this region between the tenth and the thirteenth centuries. They were supposedly moved to southeastern Transylvania for military purposes, and later on, they crossed into Moldavia, where we can still find them today. But both at the beginning and at the end of the study the author, being prudent, expresses certain reservations, which are actually the latest

---

[25]Petru Râmneanțu, *Die Abstammung der Tschangos*, Sibiu, 1944, Cf. idem, "Grupele de sânge la ceangăii din Moldova," in *Buletin eugenic și biopolitic*, XIV, 1943, nr. 1-2, pp. 51-56.

conclusions of scholars after two centuries of controversy: a) today the problem itself is still not irrevocably solved;" b) "there remain, of course, many questions to which, at present, we cannot provide any answers."[26]

Finally, Gyula Marton, in a monograph investigating Romanian lexical loans to the Hungarian Chango dialect, refrains from formulating a firm conclusion about the origins of the Changos but leaves the reader to believe that, given the langue they speak, they belong to the Magyar nation.[27] Neither Géza Bakó nor Gyula Marton mention anything about the Romanian dialect, different from the Moldavian one, spoken by the majority of the Changos.

As we can see, despite all of the research that has been carried out, there is still much confusion and uncertainty surrounding the problem of the origins of this population. However, a certain consistent line of thought can be noticed throughout this long and difficult research: the tendency to attribute to the Changos various distant, enigmatic origins; the tendency to ignore, or at least to underestimate, the evidently Romanian ethnographic elements (their costumes, their customs, their way of life), elements which could not have been borrowed in a recent epoch, but were inherited from their ancestors; the firm assertion that they supposedly borrowed their Romanian dialect from the Moldavians in a recent epoch, ignoring the specific Transylvanian character of their speech (none of the researchers asked the question: from where and from whom did the Changos inherit their Romanian dialect?).

---

[26]Bakó Géza, "Contribuţii cu privire la problema originii ceangăilor," in *Studii şi articole de istorie*, IV, 1962, pp. 37-44.

[27]Marton Gyula, *A moldvai csángó nyelvjárás roman kölcsönszavai* (*Romanian Words Borrowed by the Dialect of the Changos in Moldavia*), Bukarest, 1972, p. 603 (Editor's Note: A variant of this work was also published in Budapest, in 1950).

Scholars continued to ignore this old Romanian dialect, a mistake with serious consequences for the scholarly investigation of this problem. Most researchers held the opinion that the Changos represented, until recently, an exclusively Magyarophone population, because the fact that they speak Romanian is supposedly the result of their recent linguistic assimilation in Moldavia. The ones who taught the Changos to speak Romanian, in their specific dialect, however, could not have been the Moldavians. They had inherited this dialect from their Romanian forefathers in Transylvania. The observation made by Petru Zöld in 1766 that the Changos spoke Hungarian and Romanian equally well helps to support this hypothesis. This explains why the Magyar linguists never dealt with the Romanian dialect of the Changos. Hungarian authors have looked at the problem exclusively from a nationalist point of view. The essential problem, namely their Romanian dialect, was passed over in silence. The reader can easily imagine how the history of the Romanians in Transylvania would have remained, let us suppose if left exclusively in the hands of certain nationalist historians such as Sulzer, Roesler, Hunfalvy, and others. Such a history would have presented a distorted, incomplete image of the past of the Transylvanian Romanians, corresponding not to the historical truth, but to the political interests of Hungarian nationalists of those times. In short, the history of the Transylvanian Romanians would have been neglected. This situation is similar to that of the Changos in present-day historiography if it is permitted to compare small things with larger ones.

The old conceptions about the Changos were accepted even in Romanian historiography, so that a new interpretation of the facts from the perspective of their Romanian dialect may appear to be risky. Nevertheless, this dialect has existed for centuries; it is still spoken today, and, thus, constitutes an objective linguistic and historical fact, even though it has not been taken into consideration up to now by scholars.

Because the Romanian dialect of the Changos has been ignored in previous studies, past research has failed to elucidate any of the fundamental aspects of the problem of the origins of this population.

The Ethnic Consciousness of the Changos

On the other hand, and this is another essential element which has been neglected, despite the almost unanimous consensus of the scholars of the past and, partially, of today, who consider them an ethnic enclave of foreign origin, the Changos themselves have traditionally manifested distrust and resentment toward those who attribute such an origin to them. With the exception of some rare, individual cases,[28] these people firmly maintain that they are of Romanian origin.

Talking about the villages situated at "the gate of Târgu Frumos," north of Roman (Butea, Buruieneşti, Oţeleni, Sagna, Fărcăşeni, Rotunda, Şcheia, Slobozia, Buhonca, Boghicea, and others), the geographer Victor Tufescu noted that "almost nowhere in the villages

---

[28](Editor's Note) Such a case was that of Inocenţiu (Ince Janos) Petraş (1811-1886), a rector in Cleja (in the country of Bacău), who received a Hungarian education in Transylvania. When he returned to Moldavia as a priest, he was always hostile toward the Romanian language. However, he pointed out the spiritual values from the Romanian substratum of his parishioners, collecting the first variant of Mioriţa in Hungarian, prior to the Russo-Alecsandri classical variant (see Farago Iosif, "Variantele maghiare ale Mioriţei" – "The Hungarian Versions of Mioriţa," in *Limbă şi literatură*, V, 1961, p. 358; also Adrian Fochi, Mioriţa, Bucureşti, 1964, p. 459. About his tragic end, see Augustin Paul (Delaletca), *Între Someş şi Prut*, Bucureşti, 1905, pp. 274-275).

mentioned above can one hear Hungarian, and the so-called Changos are insulted if they are called Hungarians and not Romanians."[29]

When asked about their nationality, Cantemir's "Hungarians" avoided saying that they were Magyars, and called themselves *Catholics*,[30] a tradition preserved until today in Moldavia.[31] This is an old tradition, contemporary with Cantemir, which negates statements to the contrary by many scholars. Knowing that any popular tradition always contains some truth, a logical starting point is to ask the question: is there today or was there in the past an objective fact at the basis of the tradition that they are not Magyars? In this situation, we were helped by linguistic geography, which today has an important place in the study of language. Following the direction of these studies, we began research on the Romanian dialect of the Changos in Moldavia, unexplored by linguistics in the past and in the present. This research led us to a series of conclusions that correct older information about the Changos and shed doubt on the conclusions of Gustav Weigand and most Magyar scholars, casting new light on the language, historical past, and the origins of the Changos.

With the help of historical sources, as many as are available to us at present, and of the peculiarities characteristic of this Romanian

---

[29]Victor Tufescu, "O regiune de vie circulaţie: 'poarta Târgului-Frumos," in *Buletinul Societăţii... de Geografie*. LIX. 1940, pp. 370-371.

[30]See supra, p. 13.

[31](Editor's Note) A reference to the inhabitants of Cotnari in the county of Iaşi: "Today, if you told a Catholic from there that he is a German or Hungarian, he would answer with vexation: 'No, sir, I am a Catholic Romanian'" (Ioan Ferenţ, "Biserica veche din Cotnari," in *Calendarul catolic*, XIV, 1916, p. 39. Also Artur Gorovei, "Cotnarii în toamna lui 1930," in *Lumea*, XIII, 1930, nr. 3710, 3 noiembrie, p. 2: "A man from Cotnari who was accompanying us told us that he was a Romanian, but a Catholic." Here is the reflection of a peasant from Bârgăuani (in the county of Neamţ): "Our nationality is one with our language, and the nationality of the Hungarians is one with their language. They are a different nation." Dumitru Mărtinaş, *Caietul*, XVI, A, p. 16.

dialect, a new scientific interpretation of the ethno-linguistic Chango phenomenon in Moldavia is now possible. This is the first interpretation made from the standpoint of the Romanian dialect of the respective population and from the perspective of Romanian history. Up to now, the interpretation of this phenomenon has been considered a field reserved exclusively to Magyar linguistics, which has studied the problem only from the point of view of the Hungarian Chango dialect. Romanian scholars have never objected to this unilateral research procedure. The occasional reaction of Radu Rosetti against some propaganda articles by the Magyar publicist Tatrosi János[32] suffered from the same lack of scientific information that characterized the theses he was contesting.

The present reaction appears after many hesitations and delays.[33] For a long time, we thought it presumptuous to take a position against

---

[32]Radu Rosetti, "Une minorité ethnique imagnaire en Moldavie," in *Journel des débats* (Paris), 1922, no. 216, 6 august (Editor's Note: Tatrosi János was the pseudonym of Veress Endre, 1868).

[33](Editor's Note) "I confess that for a long time, although the conclusions of the linguistic evidence were hard to contest, I did not have the courage to rise against the formidable scholarly authority represented by the official point of view," wrote Dumitru Mărtinăş in a note from 15 October 1969. He went on to reveal the thought processes that were at the origin of this book: "1. This study was initiated due to a conscientious process: what am I, Romanian, Cuman (Weigand), or Hungarian (Philippide)? Not knowing what you are is unbearable. 2. What attitude, what stand shall I take in life, as a citizen, in my profession? Shall I look at things as a Romanian, or as a Hungarian? It is very painful for a man not to know what he is. I was suffering in my consciousness from not knowing who I was. I took notes, I began to write a novel (*Dipsihie. Omul cu două conştiinţe – Dipsihie. The Man with Two Consciences...*). No one could answer me. 3. I began searching on my own. I began learning Hungarian. I taught at Hungarian high-schools. I observed the Szeckler and the Chango students (in Transylvania). I noticed the same process with the Chango students: they avoided to admit that they were Changos, they wanted to be Szecklers, but they knew that their names were Romanian (Achim, Moldovan, Plájás), they knew that their grandparents had spoken Romanian that their uncle was *popă românesc* (a Romanian priest). The result – restlessness of the soul: I am Romanian, but I am also

such great scholars like Weigand, Xenopol. Szarvas, and others. How can one rise against the traditional conclusions of Magyar and Romanian scholarship, that is against the conclusions of well-known scientific authorities? Knowing, however, that we possess information which passes unnoticed in the past, and knowing the value of the linguistic evidence, we considered that the former conclusions drawn by scholarship concerning the origins of the Changos in Moldavia is no longer valid and that it is time that it was fundamentally reconsidered.

For any careful observer, it is obvious that the two dialects spoken today by the Changos, the Romanian and the Hungarian, are undergoing a process of gradual transformation from a linguistic point of view due to the rapid changes brought about by the influence of modern society. Fewer and fewer Changos are speaking the Hungarian dialect, until one day it will cease to exist. The Romanian Chango dialect, more widespread, is undergoing a process of progressive integration into the Moldavian dialect, and, together with the latter, into the common Romanian language. Consequently, in the near future, it will cease to exist as well. Research on both dialects, with all of the information they can provide to scholarship, is necessary and possible only in our era. Tomorrow it will be too late. This inevitable reality guided us in the elaboration of the present study.

Szeckler. Half of my face is laughing, but the other half is crying... 4. The refuge in research. I studied thoroughly the history of the Szeckler region, the Szecklerization of the Romanians. Without knowing the history of the Szecklerization of the Romanians one cannot write about the Changos. My study is the scholarly result of a struggle of decades, until I obtained scientific certainty. Now I am at peace."

Chapter 2

Old Catholic Settlements in Moldavia

It is known that Transylvania constituted, in times past, the cradle of the Romanian people in the Carpathian-Danubian region, and the demographic reservoir from which the excess pastoral and agricultural population crossed over the Carpathians into Moldavia and Wallachia.[1]

It is also known that, after taking Transylvania under its rule, the Hungarian kingdom moved a series of Catholic Magyar-Szeckler and Saxon colonists to the east of the Carpathians, as far as the valley of the Siret River, for political and military purposes, namely to stem the flow of migratory peoples from the East. These invasions from the East were quite numerous during the Middle Ages, especially in Moldavia. Their presence is often mentioned in cities and towns like

---

[1]Constantin C. Giurescu, *Transilvania in istoria poporului român*, Bucureşti, 1967, p. 47.

Siret, Baia, Suceava, Roman, Bacău, and Trotuş.[2] Many toponyms of Magyar origin (Fărăoani, Fărcaşa, Lucăceşti, Săbăoani, Tămăşeni, Timăreşti, etc.) and others of Szeckler origin (Sasca, Sascut) confirm this fact. In Wallachia, the old county of the Secuieni, meaning that of the inhabitants who had come from the Szeckler region, dissolved in 1845 and divided between the counties of Buzău and Prahova, still witnessed Szeckler infiltrations (as reflected in place names such as Calvini, Choijd, Lapoş, etc.). Here, the Szeckler population disappeared a long time ago, being assimilated by the Transylvanian Romanians and the native Romanian population, but their traces remained in the form of toponyms.[3] Numerous Magyar-Szeckler elements came from the other side of the mountains as craftsmen, merchants, and miners like the *şangăii* or the *şalgăii*.[4]

These facts are well-known by historians. What has remained unknown is that the catholic settlements in Moldavia were not inhabited by the Changos of today, but by Romanians, Magyar-Szecklers, and Saxons. The name Chango was unknown in that epoch. In 1646, neither Bandinus nor his secretary, Paul Beke, who was a Magyar, had heard of this name.

Another fact has also been overlooked. Centuries of living side by side with the native Romanian population, and all of the trials and tribulations that they endured together, resulted in the learning of the Romanian language by the Hungarians, Szecklers, and Saxons, and then in their gradual assimilation in the mass of the Romanian

---

[2](Editor's Note) See Constantin C. Giurescu, *Târguri sau oraşe şi cetăţi moldovene din secolul al X-lea până în mijlocul secolului al XVI-lea*, Bucureşti, 1967.

[3](Editor's Note) See Ecaterina Zaharescu, "Vechiul Judeţ al Saacului in lumina istoriei şi antropo-geografiei," in *Buletinul Societăţii... de Geografie*, XLI, 1922, pp. 147-173.

[4]Nicolae Iorga, "Privilegiile şangăilor de la Târgu Ocna," in *Analele Academiei Române. Memoriile Secţiunii Istorice*, seria II, volume XXXVII, 1914-1915, pp. 245-263.

population. The toponyms of foreign origin remained, but most of the respective population merged with the Romanians.[5]

---

[5](Editor's Note) Some authors argue that the present Catholic population in Moldavia has continued Latin Christianity, without interruption, from its origins until the present day (see Dominic Neculăeş, *Latinitatea bisericii româneşti*, Săbăoani-Roman, 1940, p. 72: "…we find it justified to maintain that these Catholic Moldavians, at least a small part of them, are a continuation of the Romanian remnants within the old Latin Church"). The history of Christianity among the Romanians has not been completely elucidated so far. The fact that, in 1234, Pope Grigore IX ordered Teodoric, the bishop of the Cumans, to name a bishop locum tenens of Wallachian nationality means that on the territory of this bishopric, which was directly subordinated to Rome, there were also Wallachians (Romanians) of Roman belief. Therefore, without any doubt, the papal order referring to the decisions of the council in Lateran from 1215 took into consideration first of all the local realities. Prince Laţcu of Moldavia certainly had the Romanian Catholics in view, and his action increased their number and determined the founding of the Catholic bishopric of Siret (1371), the first bishopric in the history of Moldavia. The prince did this to consolidate the international position of the new state. after his death (1375), Catholicism was supported with fervor by Margareta Muşata, the founder of the Muşat dynasty (see Ştefan Pascu, *Contribuţiuni documentare la istoria românilor in secolele XIII şi XIV*, Sibiu, 1944, p. 44; Ioan Mărtinaş, "Margareta Muşata, the founder of the Muşat dynasty" (see Ştefan Pascu, *Contribuţiuni documentare la istoria românilor în secolele XIII şi XIV*, Sibiu, 1944, p. 44; Ioan Mărtinaş, "Margareta Muşata, principesă a Moldovei," in *Almanahul "Presa Bună"*, XXXI, 1944. Pp. 61-69). In 1413, in the time of Alexander the Good, a new bishopric was founded in Baia (in 1401 the Orthodox hierarchy had been canonically organized), in 1607 the bishopric of Bacău was founded, and in 1884 the bishopric of Iaşi was founded (about the old Catholic bishopric in Moldavia, see the studies of G. Auner, mentioned in the bibliography). The Romanian element was always preponderant in Moldavian Catholicism, throughout time partially absorbing the other ethnic elements (part of these became integrated in Orthodoxy and no one ever contested their Romanian ethnic origin). He number of the Catholic Romanians increased considerably in the eighteenth century, following the massive emigrations from Transylvania, and it has been increasing ever since due to their moral and biological vitality, as well as to some conversions. If in the past the Catholic Romanians in Moldavia were very little talked about, this was due to the lack of indigenous clergy and to the protectors from outside of the Moldavian Catholic church: first of all the kings of Hungary, then the kings of Poland, and, finally, the court in Vienna, in whose conception Catholicism had to remain under foreign control to justify the need for the protectorate of Austria (see M. Theodorian Carada, *Din*

Already in 1234, this process of assimilation of the foreign population by the Romanians was recorded in a papal letter, from which we find out that on the territory of the Cuman bishopric, the Hungarians and the Saxons, merging with the Wallachians, converted to their religion, becoming one and the same people: *cum eis quasi populous unus facti.*[16] Another documentary testimony about the oldness and the intensity of this process of assimilation of the Catholic inhabitants of foreign origin is found in *Codex Bandinus*, in which the author notes that many passed to the Romanians: *ad Valachos defecere.*[7] We will not make the mistake, common to many historians, of believing that all the Moldavian Catholics between the fourteenth and seventeenth centuries were Hungarians and Saxons. Besides them, there were many Romanian Catholics as well. Out of the 1,201 Catholic families recorded nominally by Bandinus's secretary, around 300 had Romanian names. We will reproduce here a few family names from this codex: *Manul, Ciucul, Dărăbanţ, Robu, Şoltuz, Călugăr, Santa, Chinezu, Răzvan, Păcurar, Podoleanu, Blânda, Frâncu, Cioară, Cerchez, Sima, Bobacea, Biliboc, Bolha, Ciolan, Dumitraş,*

---

frământările trecutului, Bucureşti, 1920, p. 133). The rebirth of Romania also meant their rebirth to an intensive spiritual and national life. The history of the Catholic church in Moldavia forms an integral part of the history of the Romanian church.

[6]See Hurmuzaki-Densusianu, *Documente privitoare la istoria românilor*, I, Bucureşti, 1887, p. 132.

[7]V.A. Urechia, *Codes Bandinus*, Bucuresci, 1895, p. 78 (Editor's Note: The fact is also confirmed by Giulio Mancinelli, at the end of the sixteenth century: "In Moldavia he stopped a few days in Iaşi, where he found that almost all Christians were Catholics, who, a few years before, had been very numerous in the two principalities, Moldavia and Wallachia; because of the lack of Latin (= Catholic) priests they had become converted to the Greek rite (= Orthodox); even the merchants from Chios and Ragusa and from other places in Italy (had become converted), totally or to a great extent, so as not to be deprived of the religious service" (*Călători străini despre ţările române*, II, Bucureşti, 1970, p. 524; see also Cesare Alzati, *Tera romena tra oriente e occidente. Chiese ed etnie nel tardo 1500*, Milano, 1982, pp. 273-274).

Topor, Balcu, Simon, Ciorbă, Cozan, Curelar, Gâncu, Ghergu, Bălan, Roca, Damian, Dancu, Lunguţ, Balica, Sular, Butnar, Bărbuţ, Bărbos, Duma, Bogdan, Sitar, Martinel, Pascar, Sescu, Gârbea, Grosu, Cozocar, Lupu, Vernică, Moise, Lupoaie, Burcă, Busuioc, Colţea, Tulbure, Cimpoi, Cancel, Conta, Boldur, Neamţu, Budău, Bărbat, Cioban, Poarcă, Tiba, Căpitan, Barticel, Gheţu, Spânu, Tuncea, Barbălată, Brânză, Brânzoaie, Pătraşcu, Armăncuţ, Prepeliţă, Tălpălar, Nicoară, Roşca, Chişcă, Ţigan, Vinţeler, Puşcaş, Boancă, Mihăica, etc. [8] Consequently, in the seventeenth century, a great part of the Catholic population in Moldavia was Romanian. In his account, dated 1671, the Italian missionary Del Monte showed that the native language of the Moldavian Catholics was Romanian (*il vallacho e propria il nativo*), adding that the Hungarian language was necessary as well.[9] For the Romanian Catholics in Moldavia and for those of other nations who knew the Romanian language, Vito Piluzio printed in Rome a catechism with Latin characters.[10]

---

[8]Ibidem, pp. 99-129.

[9]G. Călinescu, "Alcuni missionary cattolici italiani nella Moldavia nei secoli XVII e XVIII," in *Diplomatarium italic*, I, 1923, p. 109. About Giovanni Battista del Monte, see Pr. B. Morariu, "Părintele Del Monte, un vrednic şi sfânt misionar în ţara noastră," in *Viaţa*, XXIV, 1938, nr. 4-5, aprilie-mai, pp. 69-73.

[10]Vito Piluzio, *Katekismo criistinesko*, Roma, 1677 (Editor's Note: Dottrina christiana. Tradota on lingua, valacha dal padre... is the second Romanian book printed with Latin letters and was of use both to the missionaries in Moldavia, and to the Italian scholars who wanted to learn the language (see Viorica Lascu, "Documente inedite privitoare la situaţia ţărilor române la sfârşitul secolului XVII," in *Anuarul Institutului de Istorie din Cluj*, XII, 1969, p. 238). The necessity of this Romanian catechism in the pastoring of the Moldavian Catholics is also expressed in the answer of Piluzio to a questionnaire of the Congregation of Fide Propaganda, in 1971, who confirmed the things related by Del Monte: "The Romanian language, which is the native language, is necessary, and so in Hungarian; but the Hungarians know and speak Romanian very well" (see Francisc Pall, "Le controversie tra I missionary conventuali e I gesuiti nelle missioni di Moldavia (Romania)," in *Diplomatarium italicum*, IV, 1939, p. 259).

This Catholic population never enjoyed favorable conditions for its progress. It underwent many hardships of all kinds, through many conversions to Hussitism, Lutheranism, and Orthodoxy, so that Catholicism had almost disappeared in Moldavia at the end of the seventeenth century. Even in Bandinus's time, in 1646, the area inhabited by the Catholic population was considerably reduced. What followed afterward is well-known: frequent invasions by foreign armies, plunderings by the Tartars and the taking of many inhabitants into slavery, drought, and famine, epidemics that carried off part of the population of the country, and the long Turkish-Polish war for the conquest of Camenița, with its baneful consequences for Moldavia. Those were the dreadful years Miron Costin wrote about in the preface of his chronicle: "These are terrible times, and a great ordeal for our land and for us."[11]

In a report dated 1670, Petru Parcevic, bishop of Bacău, showed that not even a third of the inhabitants from Vasile Lupu's times had remained in Moldavia. Part of them took refuge in Poland, part in Turkey, while the Catholic Hungarians had taken refuge in

---

Much has been written about the author and his work. See especially: I Bianu, "Vito Pilutio, Documente inedite din archival Propagandei," in *Columna lui Traian*, IV, 1883, nr. 1-2, ianuarie-februarie, pp. 142-149; Ramiro Ortiz, *Per la storia della cultura italiana in Romania*, Bucarest, 1916, pp. 68-85; N. Drăganu, "Catehismul din manuscrisul de la 1719 al lui Silvestru d'Amelio, copie după al lui Vito Piluzio tipărit la 1677," in *Făt-Frumos*, I, 1962, nr. 2, martie-aprilie, pp. 34-38; Josif E. Naghiu, "Despre Vito Piluzio," in *Studii și cercetări istorice*, XVIII, 1943, pp. 397-399; D. Găzdaru, "Prima tipăritură din Moldova. Contribuție la istoria culturii românești din secolul XVII," in *Buletinul Bibliotecii Române* (Freiburg), I, 1935, pp. 37-54; Giuseppe Piccillo, "Note sulla lingua valacha del Katekismo kriistinesko di Vito Pilizio," in *Studii și cercetări lingvistice*, XXX, 1979, no. 1, pp. 31-46; *Călători străini despre țările române*, VII, București, 1980, pp. 66-78. The catechism was reproduced in *Buciumul roman*, I, 1875, after the copy of Gh. Sion Gherei (A. Papiu Ilarian had also made a copy in Berlin; he had pointed out the printing for the first time in *Tesauru de monumente istorice*, I, București, 1862, pp. 105-106.

[11]Miron, Costin, *Opere*, București, 1958, p. 42.

Transsylvania.[12] And Vito Piluzio related in Rome, in 1682, that the inhabitants of some Catholic settlements were all gone (*tutti fugitti*).[13]

An example, in this sense, is the village Săbăoani, today the largest Catholic settlement in Moldavia, which was repeatedly plundered and then set on fire, and the inhabitants were scattered and forced to hide in the woods.[14] In 1682, the village suffered a terrible disaster following the Turkish and Tartar invasion. Many inhabitants were killed, others were taken into slavery by the Tartars, and those who were able to escape by running hid into the woods nearby. What was left of the village was destroyed by a new Turkish invasion in 1687, the last houses were burned down, and the old stone church, founded by Margareta Muşata,[15] was pillaged and burned down. Defenseless, the survivors who had escaped into the woods took refuge in Transylvania. For half a century, the devastated village ceased to exist. Only in 1744 other inhabitants came and settled here from the other side of the mountains, encouraged by Phanariot domination of the country. But these were not the old inhabitants who

---

[12]Auner Károly, *A romániai magyar telepek történeti vázlata* (*A Historical Outline of the Magyar Colonies in Romania*), Temesvar, 1908, pp. 40-41.

[13]I. Bianu, "Vito Pilution. Documente inedite din archivul Propagandei," in *Columna lui Traian*, IV, 1883, p. 262 (Editor's Note: See also *Călători străini*, VII, pp. 105-107. In a different report (c. 1678), it is shown, with obvious exaggeration, that Moldavia was *quasi distrutta*, the localities Cotnari, Baia, Târgu Frumos, Siret, Suceava, Botoşani, Roman, Bacău, Bârlad, Ştefăneşti, Huşi, Vaslui, and Săbăoani were deserted, their inhabitants having fled to Poland and Transylvania. Few Catholics had remained in Iaşi, Faraoani, Trotuş, and Galaţi (see G. Călinescu, *Alcuni missionari*, p. 140). V.I. Ghika maintains that, after the plunders by the Tartars, called here by the Turks, and after the plague, the number of the Catholics in Moldavia decreased at the end of the seventeenth century to 300 people (*Spicuiri istorice*, p. 20), a number which was certainly diminished compared to the real one).

[14](Editor's Note) "Săbăoani. The stone church with one altar. There is no one there," wrote Piluzio on 10 July 1682 (*Călători străini*, VII, p. 105).

[15]V.I. Ghika, *Spicuiri istorice*, Iaşi, 1936, p. 30.

had taken refuge in Transylvania; they were the Changos, the present-day inhabitants of the village. They did not settle in the old desolate precincts of the village, where the main road goes down the valley of the Siret River, but they established themselves on the plateau, near the Licuşeni forest, where they still live today.[16]

The other Catholic villages on the valley of the Siret, located near the main road of the country, the principal route taken by invading armies, had the same fate. Most of the villages were plundered, the churches were burned down, the inhabitants were killed or taken into slavery by the thousands by the Tartars, while the survivors ran away or crossed the mountains into Transylvania. Defenseless, the country fell prey to chaos and anarchy. In those times, Moldavia lost about half of its population, and the number of Catholics decreased significantly. Many of the villages mentioned in *Codex Bandinus* disappeared forever in those troubled times, while the ones that remained had a precarious existence, being deserted by most of the inhabitants.[17] When the situation calmed down, only a few of the refugees were able to come back to their old homes devastated by invasions. The few

---

[16](Editor's Note) See also P. Joseph P.M. Pal, *Schematismus fratum minorum...*, Săbăoani-Roman, 1935, pp. 32-33. In a petition lodged to the Divan in January 1768, the inhabitants of Săbăoani showed that they were unjustly submitted to statute labor, because, "being foreigners, *ungureni*," settled on the estate of the Monastery of Secu, they were only supposed to "pay half of *leu* for each harvester." But the Divan considered them inhabitants since the "founding of the village" and obliged them to do statute labor, which caused the conflict to continue over decades. See V. Mihordea, *Relaţiile agrare din secolul al XVIII-lea in Moldova*, Bucureşti, 1968, pp. 243-244.

[17]Out of the 33 localities mentioned by Bandinus, only the following have survived until today (not counting the cities): Adjudeni, Cotnari, Faraoani, Grozeşti, Răchiteni, Săbăoani, Tămăşeni, Tescani, Trebeş, Trotuş, and Valea Seacă, representing a small number compared to the over one hundred present localities with a compact or majority Catholic population. Even in these old settlements, the ethnic composition of the population was renewed and increased by numerous subsequent stratifications of population that came from the other side of the mountains.

hundred Catholic families, most of them Romanian or Romanianized, scattered throughout villages and towns in Moldavia, represented a greatly reduced percentage of the population.

How can one explain the unusual growth of the Catholic population during the next century? How did the numerous Catholic settlements, which did not exist in Bandinus's time, appear in the second half of the eighteenth century?

The answer is that it was the beginning of a new period in the history of Moldavian Catholicism due to the inhabitants who emigrated from Transylvania, in their great majority Romanians, who went through a process of Szecklerization. They, together with the converted natives, strengthened, even more, the Romanian Catholic element in Moldavia.[18]

---

[18] (Editor's Note) Ever since, the Catholic population in Moldavia has increased continuously, although the emigrations ceased at the end of the eighteenth century. Petru Râmneanțu, noticed a great disproportion in the increase of the population of Moldavia and the increase of the Catholic population here. Thus, in the period 1902-1930, the population of Moldavia increased by 37%, and the Catholic population increased with 70%; moreover, in the period 1912-1930, the former increased by 13.8%, and the latter by 42.4%. The author explains this unusual increase through an action of Catholicization (see *Problema iradierii românilor din Transilvania in principatele române*, p. 26). The explanation corresponds only partially to reality, the increase being mostly natural (see Josif Gabor, *Dicționar statistic al localităților din Moldova*, 1865-1948, vol. I-II, 673 pp. (manuscript).

Chapter 3

A New Stratification of the Population: The Changos

In the first decades of the eighteenth century, a new demographic and linguistic aspect began to take shape in Moldavia, on the valley of the Siret River. We are referring to the sudden increase of the Catholic population, through the appearance of a new demographic element: the inhabitants arrived from Transylvania, whom the Szeckler missionary Petru Zöld, in a letter from 1780 (the information dates, however, from 1766), called *Changos*, a term later adopted by Hungarian scholars. Besides some of the localities mentioned by Bandinus, which survived those "terrible times," deserted however by most of the old inhabitants, numerous new "Chango" settlements appeared. From the information we have from Petru Zöld, we know that the Changos were bilingual and dressed in Romanian costumes. Because of their Catholic religion, the Moldavians called them *Hungarians*. In their great majority, they spoke their own Romanian dialect, different from the one spoken by the Moldavians. They also spoke Hungarian, in a degraded Szeckler dialect, a mixture of Hungarian and Romanian elements, pronounced in their Transylvanian sibilant and affricate fashion. Considering their costume and their native Romanian dialect, there is no doubt that they were Transylvanian Romanians. Considering their Catholic religion, their territorial origin, and the Hungarian dialect they were speaking in certain villages, in the eyes of the Moldavians they could not be anything else but Hungarians.[1] From the beginning, these "Hungarians" appeared as a group of strange people, as the Moldavians communicated with them in Romanian. Some of them did not even know Hungarian: *Hungarians who do not know Hungarian!*[2] Due to the frequent immigration of these Transylvanians, beginning with the eighteenth century new Catholic

---

[1] (Editor's Note) "One… must also take into account the fact that the name of unguri (Hungarians) was actually used to refer to ungureni, namely Romanians from Transylvania or even Romanians from the Principalities, who had fled across the mountains and were now returning under this new name" (Constantin C. Giurescu, "Populaţia judeţului Putna la 1820," in *Buletinul Societăţii… de Geografie*, LIX, 1940, pp. 205-206. See also Sever Pop, "La dénomination de ungur, ungurean était de tradition chez les Roumains de Moldavie pour designer les Roumains venus de Transylvanie," in *Bulletin linguistique*, VIII, 1940, p. 176). In accordance with the name of the state to which it belonged at that time, Transylvania was improperly called Ţara Ungurească (the Hungarian Country) and the people who came from there were unguri (Hungarians).

[2] (Editor's Note) We mention here a coincidence. In Augustin Paul (Delaletca), Între Someş şi Prut, one of the chapters is entitled "Unguri cari nu ştiu ungureşte" (Hungarians who do not know Hungarian") (pp. 239-271). The author relates here facts and impressions from two journeys he made to Huşi, in 1897 and 1899: a woman calls a child in the street: "Măi Nyihai!," the children of the organist sing P-o stâncă neagră intr-un vechi castel, on Sundays, at the hora, the young men and women dance so beautifully that you cannot look away, and at the vespers 1,500 people sing the Lutheran litany in Romanian. The journalist was amazed by what he noticed about those "Hungarians" (he also put the term between quotation marks). If he had visited other Catholic localities in Moldavia as well, he would have probably realized that there was nothing extraordinary there, those facts being part of the everyday life of the inhabitants, who were Romanians of Catholic religion and not "Hungarians who did not know Hungarian."

villages appeared in Moldavia, especially in the northern group. Some statistics help to illustrate this demographic process:[3]

Year	Source	Numbers and Observations
1741	Stanislau Jezierski, Bishop of Bacău	8,000 recently arrived from Transylvania
1776?	Anonymous	10,620
1800	Vincenţiu Gatt, Mission Prefect	15,200 (He mentions 3,186 families with 13,514 souls, not including the parish of Săbăoani Gherăeşti
1803	Dominic Brocani, Mission Prefect	20,250 (4,033 families)

---

[3]We reconstructed the statistical data based on Pietro Tocanel, *Storia della chiesa Catollica in Romania*, III/1, Padova, [1960], Josif Gabor, *op. cit.*, pp. 10-11, and the registers of the mission and the diocese. In the manuscript, the data are reproduced from Petru Râmneanţu, *Die Abstammung der Tsangos*, pp. 19-20.

Year	Source	Numbers and Observations
1807	Hammer, Austrian Consul	21,307
1808	Aloisiu Landi, Mission Prefect	24,400
1822	Rabb, Austrian Consul	40,000
1830	Inocenţiu Pamfili, Mission Prefect	45,000 (approximately)
1841	Petru Rafael Ardiuni, Bishop	57,000
1850	Mission Report	43,587
1856	Mission Report	48,530
1874	Mission Report	58,829
1902	Diocese Report	77,335
1930	General Census of Romania	109,953

Today, the Catholics in Moldavia and Bucovina, in their great majority Romanians, number approximately 221,000 people, living in about 200 localities (according to recent church statistics).[4]

The inhabitants of the Catholic villages in Moldavia, most of them formed in the eighteenth and nineteenth centuries, are only in a small part descendants of the former population. The rapid growth of the Catholic communities was not the result of a normal demographic increase, but was due mainly to the emigration of Transylvanian Romanians, a small number of them Szecklerized, most of them in the

---

[4]This data was provided by Bishop Petru Pleşca. (Editor's Note: According to data reported by the diocese of Iaşi, on 1 January 1985, in the localities of Moldavia, with the exception of Bucovina, there were 237,000 Catholic inhabitants, plus those established in other regions of the country. the 1992 census revealed 250,179 Catholics in all the counties of Moldavia, while only 6,747 declared themselves to be Hungarians.)

process of Szecklerization. Thus, the Catholic population that remained at the end of the seventeenth century grew substantially and was renewed and strengthened by the inhabitants who came from the other side of the mountains.

They arrived in Moldavia in successive waves, especially in the eighteenth century. The emigrations into Moldavia[5] are part of a vast social-historical phenomenon of migrations, known in Transylvania under the name of *profugium Valachorum,* the massive flight of the Romanians into the two Romanian principalities, as a result of the intolerable social-economic conditions created for the serfs in Transylvania. The flight from the noblemen's estates and across the

---

5(Editor's Note) The memory of the emigrations to Moldavia, which became a kind of Elorado for the Transylvanians, is preserved in their folk poetry:

Astă-vară mi-am vărat

Sub o cetină de brad,

Dar la vară mi-oi văra

Cu mândruţa-n Moldova,

Că-n Moldova-i apă bună,

Cine bea se împreună...

Câţi voinici de seama mea

Toţi în Moldova trecea;

Câţi voinici de-a mea măsură

Toţi în Moldova trecură...

Cucul cântă, mierla zice:

Taci, nevastă, nu mai plânge,

C-o veni primăvara

Şi-om trece la Moldova,

La Moldova, ţară bună,

Unde-i naţie română...

(Ioan Urban Jarnik and Andrei Bârseanu, *Doine şi strigături din Ardeal,* Bucureşti, 1968, pp. 235, 309, 435).

border was the only possible form of reaction against the oppression and exploitation of those times. It was a real human exodus, which alarmed the public authorities of both countries. Only for the year 1767, a consular report shows that 24,000 families from Transylvania took refuge in Moldavia and Wallachia, which made the native inhabitants exclaim in astonishment: "The whole of Transylvania is coming to us!" (*Tots Transylvania ad nos venit!*).[6] The exodus of the Romanian population had taken such large proportions that the Austrian authorities took severe military measures for surveillance of the border and punishment of fugitives. Motivated by their opposition to the system of forced recruitments in the Austrian army, numerous Szeckler peasants joined the Romanians, taking refuge in Moldavia, where we still find them today, established on the valleys of the Trotuş and Tazlău rivers. But the largest group of refugees from the Szeckler region were Changos, namely the Romanians who were Szecklerized or in the process of Szecklerization. In 1763, Stanislau Jezierski, bishop of Bacău, informed the Congregation of Fide Propaganda that: *in Moldavia tot non aliter augetur numerous Catholicorum, quam per advenientes ex Transylvania Catholicos... et ideo quia Transylcani Catholici qui pertienent ad Ditionem Hungaricam... a Moldavis non vocantur Catholici, sed Hungari* ("in all of Moldavia the number of the Catholics is increasing only due to the Catholics who are coming from Transylvania... and that is because these Transylvanian Catholics belong to the Hungarian rule, the Moldavians do not call them Catholics, but Hungarians").[7]

---

[6]Augustin Bunea, *Episcopii Petru Paul Aron şi Dionisiu Novacovici sau istoria românilor transilvăneni de la 1751 la 1764*, Blaj, 1902, p. 259.

[7]G. Călinescu, "Altre notizie sui missionary cattolici nei paesi romeni," in *Diplomatarium italien*, II, 1930, p. 476. And in De Giovanni's report (1762) it is mentioned that the Catholic population had increased during the last twenty years due to fugitives from Transylvania. See G. Călinescu, *Alcuni misionari*, p. 214.

This dramatic increase in the Catholic population as a result of the emigrations from Transylvania is recorded in the same year by Iosif Cambioli, the prefect of the Catholic mission in Moldavia: "…for seven years the number of the Catholics has been increasing every day, not because the non-Catholics are converting to our religion, but because in Hungary, and especially in Transylvania, there is great famine, and now, since the conclusion of the peace between the Austrians and the Prussians, soldiers are recruited by force and that is why entire families[8] and a large number of young people aged 14 and older, because this is the age they begin recruiting them, are coming to this province… Having in view the increase in number of the Catholics during the last four years, in two villages in Moldavia two Catholic churches have been built, the biggest and most beautiful ones,

---

[8]The aversion to forced recruitments into the army can also be noticed after they settled in Moldavia. For this reason, on 24 April 1831 there was a fierce fight between the Tsarist troops and the peasants in Săbăoani, helped by those in the neighboring areas, among whom there were Orthodox believers as well (at the same time there took place peasant uprisings in other parts of Moldavia as well; see Gh. Duzinchevici, "Răscoalele din Moldova în anul 1831 împotriva Regulamentului Organic," *Revista Arhivelor*, V/2, 1943, pp. 352-366; about Săbăoani, see pp. 356-357). Casualties: 2 Tsarist officers, 30 Catholic peasants from Săbăoani, 4 from Pildeşti, 3 from Gherăieşti, 1 from Barticeşti, 1 from Prăjeşti (in the country of Bacău), and 5 Orthodox peasants from different villages; after a few days 35 of the wounded died (see Iosif Gabor, "Lupta de la Săbăoani dintre săteni şi armata ţaristă, 24 aprilie 1831," p. 14, manuscript; according to the data communicated by the author, in a letter dated 8 April 1980, Petru Sescu-Păduraru wrote an article on this subject and sent it to the *Korunk* journal in Cluj-Napoca, where it was published under the signature of Erdös Szászka Péter, translated, presented, and completed by István Imreh; see no. 3/1982, pp. 222-224). Also P. Felix Wiercinski S.J., "Din trecutul satului Săbăoani," in *Almanahul "Presa Buna,"* XVII, 1930, pp. 69-71. When the army became a national one, this aversion disappeared completely, and the children of those who fell in Săbăoani would be brave soldiers and would write glorious pages in the War for Independence (a peasant from Gherăieşti, for example, came home from Plevna with seven medals and, among other trophies, he brought a Turkish sword, which is now exhibited at the museum in Iaşi; see Ioan Mărtinas, "Gherăieşti, sat de frunte în ţinutul Romanului," ibidem, XXVIII, 1941, p. 53).

the best we have built in this mission: one in Hălăuceşti and the other in Talpa; in Hălăuceşti there are approximately 60 families, and in Talpa over 70 and 30 in the neighboring areas, all of them Catholic; there are also many families that have just arrived and decided to build houses there."[9]

In 1777, Antonio Mauro, prefect of the mission, wrote to Prince Grigore Ghica about the emigration and immigration of the population, specifying that the Catholic priests had brought many Transylvanians and Hungarians to Moldavia where they helped them settle: *icon vantaggio dei Serenissimi Principi*.[10]

We have another report of Antonio Mauro, dated 1782, about the presence in Moldavia of the Greek-Catholic Transylvanians: "There are also Uniate Moldavians (Romanians) in the area of Valea Seacă and it would be good for their souls if the bishop of Blaj, in Transylvania, were ordered to send a Uniate priest, and also an aide for the latter, although some of the Uniate Moldavians go to our church."[11] The various difficulties that the Greek-Catholic Church in Transylvania was going through, at that time under the leadership of Bishop Grigore Maior, did not allow for the fulfilment of this request. In the absence of their own clergy, the Greek-Catholic Romanians in Moldavia were assimilated, over time, by the Orthodox or Roman-Catholic religions, depending on the villages in which they settled.

From the reports of the missionaries it results that besides the heavy economic burdens, which determined the Romanian peasants, and sometimes the Szecklers as well, to search for the hidden paths of the mountains to take refuge in Moldavia, there was the new

---

[9] G. Călinescu, Altre notizie," p. 474.

[10] Nicolae Iorga, *Studii şi documente*, I-II, Bucureşti, 1901, p. 115.

[11] Iosif Petru M. Pal, *op. cit.*, pp. 48-49. See also the previous report in G. Călinescu, *op. cit.*, p. 513.

misfortune of the forced military service, introduced by the Austrian authorities. In the plans of the political leaders in Vienna, the annexation of Transylvania and, later, of Bucovina, had the purpose, among others, to increase the manpower of the imperial army. Consequently, thousands of young Romanians and Szecklers were recruited by force in the army and sent to fight on different fronts, where they were sacrificed for the interests of the Hapsburg Empire. This caused deep grief and revolt among the Romanian and Szeckler populations. Having no other possibility of escaping, the inhabitants of the villages, especially the young people, facing all sorts of dangers, as the borders were carefully guarded, would cross the border in large groups into Moldavia and Wallachia, where they escaped the terror of the odious forced recruitments, and were even welcomed by the authorities, who offered them certain exemptions and economic benefits, and better living conditions. This can be easily explained: the numerous estates held by the prince, boyars, and the monasteries remained untilled and unproductive because of the lack of manpower.

If historians in the past and many of those in the present have considered the Changos, with whom many Greek-Catholic Romanians are mixed, to be a population of non-Romanian origin, although they have long given up and forgotten the Hungarian language, this is due, in large measure, to linguistic misinformation, to the lack of knowledge and study of their Romanian dialect inherited from their Transylvanian Romanian ancestors. History could not preserve a more convincing document, a more evident proof of their Romanian origin, than this traditional dialect.

It is true that, in the eyes of public opinion, all the Catholic inhabitants of Moldavia, regardless of their nationality, were considered to be Hungarians, using the criterion of their religion. The public in Moldavia was not at all informed regarding the process of Szecklerization in Transylvania. Not even the scholars of those times knew the historical causes and conditions that gave birth to the Chango phenomenon. Certainly the Phanariot administration did not manifest any interest or understanding for the tragic destiny of these people who were coming by the thousands from the other side of the mountains. The Changos were survivors of a painful episode in Transylvanian Romanian history, but no one saw in them anything but economic instruments destined to provide cheap manpower for the vast boyar estates, to pay tributes, and to perform statute labor. Being appreciated for their diligence and therefore necessary for the economy of the country, they were encouraged to establish themselves in Moldavia, but the state did not lend them a helping hand very often. They were generally regarded as foreigners and left on their own.

Chapter 4

Petru Zöld about the Changos

Together with the rich correspondence of the Italian missionaries in Moldavia, one of the most valuable sources of information regarding the Catholic inhabitants of Moldavia, their dialect, and their costume, are three letters of the missionary Petru Zöld:

1. Notitia de rebus hungarorum qui in Moldavia et ultra degant, scripta Adm. R.D. Petro Zold parocho Csik-Delmensi in Siculia data ad A.R.P. Vicenti Blaho;[1]

2. His letter addressed to Ignaţiu Batthyáni, bishop of Transylvania, dated 11 January 1781;[2]

3. His letter addressed to Andrei Dudassi, a Pauline monk, dated 3 June 1787;[3]

---

[1]Written in 1780, it was published in Ungarisches Magain (Pressburg), III, 1783, no. 1, pp. 90-110 (in German version under the titles "Reise nach der Moldau") and in Molnár János, Magyar koniv-haz, III, Posonyban, 1783, pp. 414-428 (Hungarian version).

[2]Written in Latin and published in Veszley, Imets és Kovács, *Utazasa Moldva Olahhonban* 1868, *Maros-Vasarhelyt*, 1870, pp. 57-66 (part III; each part of the volume has separate numbering); it was translated into Magyar by Domokos Pál Péter, op. cit., pp. 52-60.

[3]We have no information of it having ever been published; the original in Latin is preserved in the Secret Archives of the Vatican, the Garampi Fond, volume 96, R. 25, m. 250-253. We are in the possession of a copy made by Professor Dumitru Zaharia from Bacău. (Editor's Note: We received a copy through the kindness of Dumitru

Petru Zöld was a Szeckler, born in Madefalău, today called Siculeni (in the country of Harghita).[4] Having contact with Romanians since he was young, he became accustomed with their dialect, as spoken in that region. As a priest, he cared very much for his people, knew their problems, and sympathized with them.

An active participant in the social and political events of his times, in 1763 Zöld stood up for the Szecklers who were protesting against the forced recruitments imposed by the Austrians. Coming into conflict with the state authorities, he was tried, sentenced as agitator, and imprisoned in Alba Iulia. After one year of detention, he managed to escape and took refuge in Moldavia, where he remained for five years, until the granting of political amnesty (1770), when he returned home.

In *Notitia* and in his letter addressed to Bishop Batthyáni, written many years after the conclusion of his missionary activity during his refuge, he provides a great deal of information about the ecclesiastical

---

Zaharia and Martin Bursuc (from Bacău), to whom we are grateful. A passage from the letter contains data regarding the Moldavian mission. One observes the same accusations against the Italian missionaries, who did not know and therefore never preached in the Hungarian language, but only in Romanian, the latter being cognate to Italian and therefore easier for them to learn; they did not preach in Romanian very well either, using many Italian words, so that the pure Hungarians did not understand anything, and those who spoke Romanian understood very little. There was no parish that could not be administered by a priest who spoke not only Hungarian, but the knowledge of Romanian was more convenient: Nulla vero ex doictis parochiis quam non solius hungaricvae linguae quarus sacerdos administrare possit, pro commodiori enim est linguae valachicae peritia).

4(Editor's Note) Some biographical data in Bitay Arpád, "Zöld Péter, egyénisége" ("The personality of Petru Zöld"), in *Erdélyi irodalmi szemle*, IV, 1927, pp. 165-172. In Madefalău, on 7 January 1764, the well-known *siculicidum* (the massacre of the Szecklers) took place, followed by the emigration of some Szecklers in Moldavia (see Teodor Chindea, "Siculicidum," in *Gazeta Ciucului*, IV, 1932, nr. 14, 1 septembrie, pp. 1-3; Adrian Hamzea, "Gesta siculorum, IV, Urgia de la Siculeni," in *Astra*, XVII, 1983, nr. 4, aprilie, p. 6.

situation of the Catholics in Moldavia. As a clergyman and a Szeckler patriot, the former missionary expressed his concern about the uncertain future of the Magyar language in that country. He criticized the pastoral activity of the Italian missionaries, who were never very well thought of by Magyar missionaries, because the Italians did not support them in their tendencies of Magyarization. The parishioners in most of the villages, whom Zöld called Changos and considered Magyars, were indifferent toward the Magyar language. Although in the past, in Transylvania, they had experienced a process of Szecklerization and had learned the Magyar language, in Moldavia most of them were speaking Romanian and little or no Hungarian.

For most of them, the process of Szecklerization had been superficial and had not taken root in their linguistic consciousness; their native language, the language used in their homes, had remained Romanian, the language in which they could express themselves most easily. The Magyar language was being used only by the inhabitants of some villages, especially in the region of Bacău, who had been through a more advanced process of Szecklerization. The Italian missionaries, who had been entrusted with the pastoring of the Moldavian Catholics, did not usually succeed in learning the Magyar language; they used the Romanian language, which was closer to their own: *un linguaggio facilissimo... composto piu del latino e dell'italiano che d'atra lingua* ("a very easy language... composed rather of Latin and Italian than another language").[5] In their missionary activity, as well as in their writings, (sermons, catechisms, conversation textbooks),[6] the Italians used the Romanian language.

---

[5] G. Călinescu, *Alcuni missionary*, p. 214.

[6] (Editor's Note) About the Romanian writings of the Italian missionaries, see: Carlo Tagliavini, "Alcuni manoseritti rumeni sconosciuti di missionary cattolici italiani in Moldavia (sec. XVIII)," in *Studi rumeni*, IV, 1929-1930, pp. 41-104; D. Găzdaru, "Informaţii italiene inedite despre câteva texte româneşti scrise de misionari

They also used Romanian in their extra ecclesiastical relationships with their parishioners. Under these circumstances, it was easy to see that the future of the Hungarian language would be compromised in Moldavia unless the population was compelled, by every possible means, to use the Magyar language at home and especially in church, something which history fully confirmed.

Apart from some unimportant historical notes about the communities in the Moldavian mission, Zöld also recorded some interesting information about the language and costumes of the catholic inhabitants. Unfortunately, this information remained almost unknown, as historians overlooked it or used it only partially.

To understand the information given by Petru Zöld, we must mention that the Catholic population of certain villages (for example Hălăuceşti and Talpa) settled here in 1756, that is only ten years before the visit of the Szeckler missionary, as is stated in his report to Iosif Cambioli, the prefect of the mission.[7]

The First Documentary Mention of the Name Chango

As we have previously stated, the first documentary mention of the name *Chango* is found in Petru Zöld's *Notitia*, written in 1780 and published in German translation three years later. This first mention appears under the form *csángó-magyar* and refers to the Catholic inhabitants of Moldavia, who, in Zöld's opinion, were a mixture of Hungarian and Szecklers. They are now referred to in this way without

---

catolici," in *Studii italiene*, I, 1934, pp. 79-89 (see also *Omagiu profesorului D. Găzdaru*, I, Freiburg, 1974); P. Bonaventura Morariu, "Bibliografia franciscană în Moldova," in *Almanahul... "Viaţa"*, 1925, pp. 53-59 (signed P.M.); Iosif Petru M. Pal, op. cit., pp. 233-240.

[7] See supra, p. 25.

knowing why and who gave them this name.[8] This denomination is also mentioned in the letter to Bishop Battyáni (1781), in the form of *csángó-magyarok*, without mentioning that its origin is not known. The author does not mention anything directly about the Romanians. In both his letters he shows, however, that all these inhabitants spoke Romanian and Hungarian, and that they spoke Hungarian very badly;[9] in *Notitia* he also mentions that they wore Romanian clothes made by their women.

The late documentary appearance of the term *Changos* is not accidental.[10] This name was given to their mixed Hungarian idiom, called *csángó-beszéd* (hybrid language), from the Hungarian verb *csángani* (to hybridize).[11] The name was extended from this mixed dialect to its speakers, who were called *csángók*. This is easy to understand: the Changos, being Romanian, could not pronounce certain sounds of the Magyar language, and that is why they replaced them with similar Romanian sounds, which sounded unpleasantly to the ears of the Szecklers. They pronounced the Hungarian dialect according to the Romanian basis of hearing and articulation.

The Hungarian dialect of the Changos appeared during the process of Szecklerization in southeastern Transylvania, and not in Moldavia, as results from Zöld's account. It was brought to Moldavia

---

[8]Reise nach der Moldau, p. 96.

[9](Editor's Note) In contrast with the very clear characterization of the Hungarian pronunciation by the Changos (multo blesius, respectively sehr unangenehm), Gyula Márton wrote: "Zöld mentions among other things that the Changos understand equally well the Hungarian language and the Romanian language, but they speak Hungarian better" (see "Câteva aspecte ale bilingvismului maghiaro-român la ceangăii din Moldova," in *Studii şi cercetări linvistice*, XII, 1961, nr. 4, p. 541; the author quotes the Hungarian version published by Molnár János).

10 About the attestation of the term, see Mikecs László, op. cit., p. 358.

11 See Aladár Ballagi's explanation, infra, p. 36.

by its speakers only in the eighteenth century, during the emigration waves from the other side of the Carpathians.

Geographic Origin

Zöld does not specify the geographic origin of the Changos. About the Szecklers who settled in Moldavia after the massacre of Madefalău (1764), he says that they were originally from the regions of Ciuc, Giurgeu, and Trei Scaune.[12] That is where most of the Changos were also originally from. Ştefan Meteş shows that some were from the regions of Năsăud and Dăbâca.[13] The fact that most of them were originally from the Szeckler region is also confirmed by the register of the monastery of Şumuleu-Ciuc from 1763, in which the Moldavian Catholic pilgrims are mentioned, who came there for the dedication day; they are described as being *e Siculia originate* and wearing white clothing (*albis induti vestibus*),[14] which, it is known, is characteristic of the Romanians.[15] The register does not mention,

---

[12]Veszley, Imets és Kovács, op. cit., p. 61.

[13]Ştefan Meteş, *Emigrări româneşti din Transylvania în secolele XIII-XX*, ed. II, Bucureşti, 1977, p. 168.

[14]Iosif Petru M. Pal, op. cit., p. 47.

[15](Editor's Note) See Alexandru Odobescu: "...I have to point out here, where we have talked about the white garments of the Dacians, a distinctive character of the Romanian costume. The Romanians wear white, both in summertime and in wintertime; white is the predominant color with them; and notice that no other European people has this predilection for the color of purity, as a great Romanian poet said a few years ago" (*Artele în România*, Bucureşti, 1924, pp. 62-63). The same remark was made by Mihail Sadoveanu: "The Romanian people has preserved since ancient times its white costume, which means propriety and purity" ("Câteva note," in *Viaţa românească*, XVII, 1964, nr. 4-5, aprilie-mai, p. 12).

however, what language these pilgrims from Moldavia were speaking.[16]

Nationality

As a Szeckler, Zöld saw the Changos as a Magyar population (*csángó-magyar*) that resulted from intermixing with the Saxons, who had disappeared.

The Moldavians of those times also considered the Catholic Changos to be a Hungarian population. In those times, religious identity was equated with national identity. According to the same criterion, and to the custom of the country, even the Italian missionaries called their parishioners *hungari* and *ungheresi*. The Italians were not used to differentiate between the notion of Hungarian (*ungur)* and that of *ungurean* (another name for Transylvanian). And even if they had discerned this difference, neither the Latin nor the Italian language had any corresponding terms. After a series of details related by Zöld, as well as by the Italian missionaries, we easily realize that there was no Magyar ethnic belonging, but only the belonging to the Catholic religion, considered a Hungarian religion in those times.[17]

---

[16]The tradition of the pilgrimage to Şumuleu was preserved until recent times (it is said that the statue of Madonna that is found here was brought from the monastery of the Franciscans in Bacău). The pilgrims would walk there, singing in Romanian. About the pilgrimage of 1931, the journal Viaţa informs us: "All those who would meet this group of pilgrims were amazed, especially because all the prayers and the songs that they sung were Romanian" (XVII, 1931, nr. 6, iunie, p. 111).

[17]The term *Hungarian* being equivalent to *Catholic,* often the Italian missionaries appear in documents as Hungarians: "the Hungarian priest Felicsi Antonio Zaulu" (see Nicolae Iorga, *Studii şi documente,* I-II, p. 91) was the Italian Felix Antonio Zauli, the author of a catechism and a gospel book in Romanian. The equivalence *Catholic=Hungarian* is unfortunately still preserved today (for the Hungarians, on the contrary, the two terms are not synonyms, because the Protestant religion is considered especially *magyar vallás*). Therefore it is not surprising that the writer

In the eyes of the Moldavians, the Changos, being Catholics, could not be anything else but Hungarians. One thing confused them however: the current language of these "Hungarians" was Romanian, and some of them did not know Hungarian. Their women were skilled at charming away illnesses in Romanian and at mourning for the dead, also in Romanian. Sometimes, the Moldavian women, when they wanted to learn old counter-charms, appealed to the *unguroance* old women, skilled in this area.[18] The following question arises: how

---

Cezar Petrescu said about his sister, who had become converted to Catholicism and was a nun become *unguroancă* (the paper by Iosif E. Naghiu; around the conversion of Ştefania Petrescu, Archimandrite Iuliu Scriban initiated a polemic in the newspaper *Cuvântul* of 17 October 1930, to which the following participated: Nae Ionescu, known for his exclusivist thesis, Iosif Frollo, Em. Serghie, Madeleine Winkler, the daughter of Ioan Ionescu de la Brad, etc.; see Iosif Frollo, *Românism şi catolicism*, Bucureşti, 1931). We relate here a recent funny incident: seeing a group of black students coming out of a Roman-Catholic church on a Sunday, a woman exclaimed in bewilderment to another: "What, now the black people are Hungarian nationality, which is false. The procedure "is unfair and dangerous and in contradiction with reality" (Dumitru Mărtinaş, "Eroarea cărturarilor nostril," in *Caietul Alfa*, I, p. 145).

[18]In his short story *Credinţă strămoşească*, Mihail Sadoveanu (the writer was first baptized by the Catholic priest in Paşcani) describes a halt, in the night of Saint Andrew, at a peasant in Săbăoani, who greets the guests this way: "Welcome, welcome! How are you *zupâne Ilie?*" and goes "into a clean room, full of wall carpets, and a pile of clothes adorned with flowers by the stove," with "Catholic icons with icon lamp" that filled half of the eastern wall. "The face of *lelea* Nuţa was lost in the steam of the food, with her smile and with her dark eyes. Her words remained imprinted in my mind, their sound, their modulations. When I was a child I always had an indefinite fear of those plump women, with tight *catrinţă* and big, white kerchief, stretched on *coarne* (horns)... The old women in our village would use them in their magic; the *unguroaice* were mistresses over all the secrets, the destinies, and spells of the darkness..." ("Ţi-aduci aminte," in *Opere*, VIII, Bucureşti, 1953, pp. 539, 541). Two customs are also mentioned: a) the smearing of the windows with garlic in the night of Saint Andrew (p. 542; see *Cronica Parohiei Barticeşti*, VII, p. 171: "...all of them would smear with garlic the doors, the windows, the corners of the house, the gate; b) the stabbing of the wraith with the stake driven into the grave (p. 544). Two corrections: the correct word is unguroance, as Mărtinaş writes, not unguroaice; lelea Nuţa, "who was whispering a disenchantment" when the grandson of zupânul Ilie

should one interpret the fact that the "Magyar" Changos, who had just arrived from the Szeckler region, used the Romanian language at home, and sometimes *only* the Romanian language? One would have expected them, if they were really Hungarians, to speak Hungarian at home. The cause of the apparent anomaly was the following: the Magyar mentioned by the missionary Zöld were, in fact, Romanians, and it was only because of their Catholic religion that they were called Hungarians. From the point of view of their nationality and mother tongue they were Romanians. In Transylvania of those times, the conversion to Catholicism conferred upon the respective citizen the official position of Magyar. In actual fact, however, these "Magyars" continued to live according to their traditions and customs and to speak their native language. Their linguistic integration took place over the course of time, and their total assimilation, namely the loss of their specific ethnic features, was a long process. After settling in Moldavia, despite being called Hungarians, the Changos lived according to their ancient ethnic traditions: language (most of them), national costume, customs, traditions, and way of life (all of them). For these reasons, it is clear that they are of Romanian nationality and ethnic origin,

---

awoke, is Niţa, a traditional woman's first name (Ana). About the coarne (horns) and their spreading area, see Ion Chelcea, "Portul 'cu coarne,'" in *Studii şi cercetări Muzeul Satului*, 1970, pp. 143-164. Those written by the author regarding the disenchantments are confirmed by Maria Spiridon from Mirceşti (in the county of Iaşi), who declared that she learned a disenchantment from an "old unguroanci" (Emil Petrovici, *Texte dialectale*, Sibiu-Leipzig, 1943, p. 208). These old magic practices gave a lot of trouble to the missionaries. The questionnaire regarding the confession in *Diverse materie in lingua Moldova* by Antonio Mauro (1797) includes references to disenchantments as well: Am dechentat de obranz, de adochiat, de scerpe, de dragoste sci am crezut la dischentici che folosek (Carlo Tagliavini, op. cit., p. 79).

even though, due to historical circumstances, many of them went through a more or less profound process of Szecklerization. Our conclusion corresponds to the fact that they also consider themselves Romanians.

Romanian-Hungarian Bilingualism

Petru Zöld's trip to the Catholic villages in Moldavia took place in 1766. As we mentioned previously, the inhabitants he encountered had established themselves in these villages only in the middle of the eighteenth century, that is approximately ten years before the visit of the Szeckler missionary. What did Zöld ascertain about the language of these inhabitants? "All of them know and speak equally well both Romanian and Hungarian" (*Omnes linguam moldavicam sive valachicam aeque av hungaricam et callent, et loquuntur*).[19] This statement is a very valuable source of knowledge about the Changos in the eighteenth century. It demonstrates that, in 1766, the Changos visited by the Szeckler missionary were bilingual. Thus, these "Hungarians" spoke Romanian as well. The question naturally arises, were they Magyars or not?

Without any doubt, the Changos could not have been assimilated by the Moldavians in one decade, between 1756, the date of their settling in Hălăuceşti, for example, and 1766, when they were visited by Zöld. As history has demonstrated numerous times, such a process of assimilation requires a much longer period of time. Logically, we must conclude that their bilingualism developed in Transylvania, predating their arrival in Moldavia.

The social and political circumstances in the Szeckler region of those times being known, we can maintain with certainty that it was

---

[19]Veszley, Imets és Kovacs, op. cit., p. 58.

not the Romanians who assimilated the Szecklers, but, on the contrary, the dominant nation Szecklerized the Romanians, whom afterwards, because of their mixed Hungarian language, they named, *csángók*, that is a sort of hybrids. Therefore, initially, the Changos were a population of Szecklerized Transylvanian Romanians.

The Changos studied by Petru Zöld spoke Romanian because they were Romanians, and they spoke broken Hungarian, as we will see, because they were Romanians going through a process of Szecklerization, which was not fully completed.

Zöld's finding that all Changos spoke Romanian is very significant. In addition to this there is the attestation of Hrisostomo de Giovani who, in 1762, stated that all the missionaries in this region spoke Romanian, and for the training of the pastors no other language but Romanian was used, except for the teaching of the catechism, which, in some places, is done in Hungarian as well.[20] These affirmations confirm, in an unexpected way, Zöld's finding.

Could those people be Magyars Romanianized in Moldavia in a single decade, from 1756 until 1766, or were they Transylvanian Romanians in a process of Szecklerization, who were using their traditional Romanian language? Had they been Magyars, as Zöld considered them, they would represent a unique case in history of some Magyars who spoke Romanian immediately after settling in Moldavia.

Consequently, the Changos of 1766 were, without any doubt, Transylvanian Romanians. They were considered Magyars as they were of Catholic religion and undergoing a process of Szecklerization. The method used with the Romanian serfs was simple: first they were convinced to convert to Catholicism or Protestantism, and then they

---

[20]G. Călinescu, op. cit., p. 214.

were declared "Magyars". This was what happened to the Changos met by Zöld in Moldavia.

With regard to the bilingualism of these inhabitants, Zöld offers some interesting data. About their language, he specifies that they spoke Hungarian in a very lisping way (*loquuntur hungaricam multo blesius*).[21] Why did Zöld's "Hungarians" speak Hungarian in a lisping, sibilant way? This detail is revealing. This phenomenon is characteristic of certain local Transylvanian Romanian dialects, as we will see later, but was unknown in the Magyar phonetical tradition. The Szecklerized Changos inherited this pronunciation from their sibilant Romanian dialect from Transylvania, which had been their native language.

In *Notitia*, Zöld shows that the Changos spoke the Magyar language in a very unpleasant way, with their old simplicity (*sehr unangenehm, nach ihrer alten Einfalt*).[22] This old phonetical tradition, characteristic to the Romanians, was unknown in the Magyar phonetical tradition. Being unable to pronounce certain Hungarian sounds which were difficult for the Romanians, they transposed in their new adopted language the pronunciation practices of their old Romanian language: the sibilant pronunciation, the affrication of the dental consonants /t/, /d/, the pronunciation of the Magyar affricate /cs/ /c/ as /s/ (for example *sont* instead of *csont*, like *soban, socoi* in the Moldavian dialect and in some Transylvanian dialects).

Zöld's findings are clear in this respect. It is unfortunate, however, that, up to now, scholars have neglected them.

---

[21]Veszley, Imets és Kovács, *op. cit.,* p. 58.

[22]*Reise nach der Moldau,* p. 97.

The Costume

As supplementary information, Petru Zöld records an ethnographic detail, illustrative of the nationality of these inhabitants: "Their clothing is Romanian, cheap, and is made by their wives" (*Ihe Kleidung ist walachisch, nicht kostbar und ein Werkihrer Weiber*).[23] This information is confirmed by the above-mentioned register of the Monastery in Şumuleu-Ciuc, which tells about the pilgrims arriving from Moldavia "dressed in white garments" (*albis induti vestibus*), namely in traditional Romanian costume. The wearing of this costume is another unmistaken indication of their Romanian ethnic origin.[24]

Synthesizing Zöld's findings, we reach the following conclusions: the Changos visited by him were at that time bilingual, speaking Romanian and broken Hungarians, and were wearing traditional Romanian costumes. The findings of the missionary date from 1766, that is from precisely the time of their settling in Moldavia, when any process of assimilation by the Moldavians is out of the question. Such a massive process of language and costume assimilation, within the limits of a decade, is inconceivable. The Moldavians of those times could not have taught the presumed Hungarians to speak Romanian in

---

[23] Ibidem.

[24] (Editor's Note) In the past, a well-developed domestic textile industry existed in their villages. All kinds of things were woven: carpets, rugs, thick long coats, cloth for trousers, sacks, girdles, peasant skirts, and cotton cloth of spun yarn or striped, which was bleached at the brook and then folded. Even today old women keep a pair of girdles at the bottom of trunks (in fact only a single piece, with fringes at its ends), a peasant skirt, a burial gown, and a piece of cloth for lowering the coffin into the grave. They never wear these things, treasuring them as their conscious memento mori and saving them for the day when they fold their hands on their chests... As a belief from ancient times has it, the burial clothes are those in which one will resurrect on Judgement Day and on no account would old women want to come back to life wearing other apparels than those they were dressed in when they passed away, that is, the attire of yore.

a Transylvanian dialect and to lend them their Romanian costume in a variant different from their own.

This is why the thesis regarding the linguistic assimilation and the Romanianization of the Changos, favored by many, collapses by itself. The Changos of those times, as well as today, spoke and speak Romanian in their specific Transylvanian dialect, *not* because they were assimilated by the Moldavians, but because they were of Transylvanian Romanian origin. This was no secret to the Szecklers. They had lived together with them and they certainly knew what the nationality of the Changos was. Nevertheless, many authors maintain that they are Hungarians. How can such an unscholarly attitude be explained? The explanation is of a political nature. The Hungarian state of the old days, in which the dominant nation represented a numerical minority, was permanently in need of Magyars, and thus tried to produce them artificially. The assimilation of other nationalities was one of the major concerns of Hungarian policy in the past. In conformity with this traditional policy, the Romanians, who in southeastern Transylvania initially formed the majority of the population, were the first group targeted. Their civil and political rights, together with their properties were gradually taken away, especially after *Unio trium nationum* (1438); they were made serfs and subjected to a long process of Szecklerization. According to the official interpretation, one who was a Catholic was *eo ipso* a Magyar, regardless of his language and ethnicity, and thus the Catholic Romanians were legally considered to be Magyars.[25] This is why some

---

[25]In his paper entitled *La Transilvania* (1583), "The first systematic historical, geographical, political, and religious treaty about Transylvania" (George Lăzărescu, *Repere de cultură*, Bucureşti, 1982, pp. 41-42), the Italian Jesuit Antonio Possevino, a famous missionary and diplomat, also refers to "Citulia", "a part of Dacia which stretches to Moldavia's boundaries," peoples by "Scituli" (Szecklers) and by "many Romanians," remarking that "more vestiges of Catholicism can be found in this province than in the entire Transylvanian land... especially in the capitals of Ciuc,

historians energetically defended the thesis according to which the Changos, being Catholics, were Hungarians. Thus, for instance, Lászlo Mikecs, while admitting that they are not Szecklers, nevertheless argues that they are Magyars. These authors could not ignore the fact that the Changos in Moldavia speak Romanian, wear Romanian costumes, have Romanian costumes, and live according to the Romanian way of life. Facing this undeniable set of facts, they formulated a new thesis, namely that they were denationalized and assimilated linguistically by the Moldavian Romanians, in a recent period. Although this thesis was easy to disprove, Romanian linguists and historians neglected to study the problem.

The thesis of their assimilation by the Moldavians is old, especially in Hungarian scholarship and journalism. Ever since Elek Gegö's time (1838), but especially since Gábor Szarvas's time, it has been maintained that the Changos were Romanianized and taken away from the Magyar nation. This thesis is widespread, but does not conform to the scholarly evidence.

The Mother Tongue

As we have previously shown, the bilingualism of the Changos did not come into being in Moldavia, but originated in Transylvania, as a result of the Szecklerization of the Romanians. Zöld did not

---

Gurghiu, and Casson. They all speak Hungarian, except the Romanians who live among them" (*Călători străini*, II, pp. 551-552, 554). The author does not refer at all to the religion endorsed by the Romanians who used to live here, and we can thus infer that most of them were Catholics, otherwise he would have mentioned that their faith was Greek or that they were "schismatics". The influence of the Szecklers' language would be felt later, being exerted gradually, not only upon the Catholics, but on the Greek-Catholic people as well (after 1700). This process did not entail a change in religion.

mention, however, which was their mother tongue. The reports of the Italian missionaries clarify this important detail, when they refer to the language necessary for communicating with the Catholic population in Moldavia: *non si usa altra lingua che la moldava.*[26] Thus their preferable language was Romanian, in which they listened to the sermon, sand, prayed, confessed their sins to the priest, and talked among themselves and with the other inhabitants of the country.

It is still puzzling that although his information and the resulting conclusions plead for the Romanian nationality of the Changos, Zöld considers them to be Magyars, a thesis taken up by many later authors. This contradiction has its explanation in the political conceptions of those times, according to which a citizen, regardless of his ethnicity, once he became converted to one of the religions considered to be Magyar, he became a Magyar. That is the authorities considered you Magyar if you were Catholic or Protestant, regardless of your ethnicity.[27]

In Moldavia, the situation was completely changed. Here, the laws of Transylvania did not hold authority. Although the Moldavians considered the Catholic inhabitants to be Hungarians as well, because of their religion they were, however, free to choose. And they chose to be Romanians, like their ancestors. The Magyar ecclesiastical and civil authorities soon found out that the Changos established in Moldavia did not wish to speak Hungarian any more, that most of them spoke only Romanian, and that the Magyar language was being forgotten in most of the villages and was disappearing. The reports of the Magyar missionaries, which include Zöld's letters, confirm these facts. The authorities, especially the Church, became alarmed, made

---

[26]G. Călinescu, *Alcuni missionary,* p. 214.

[27]The demographic statistics were calculated according to denominations, not nationalities.

representations to Rome, sent emissaries to Moldavia did everything in their power for the unaltered preservation of the Catholic religion.[28] But the realities in Moldavia did not coincide with those in Transylvania. Neither the Italian missionaries, nor the civil authorities had any interest in supporting the cultivation of the Magyar language and therefore the continuation of the process of Szecklerization. This language had lost any political significance and was no longer necessary because most of the Changos were speaking only Romanian. The linguistic reality today further confirms that their mother tongue was Romanian.

---

[28]This was the major reason invoked by some Magyar missionaries, who considered that their presence here was absolutely necessary (Toma Possoni, for instance, who had been banished from Moldavia for immortality, wrote on 11 April 1791: Hinc hungarici curatores animarum in Moldavia ita sunt necessari, sicut panis quotidianus, sine illis autem ineffabile animarum detrimentum, et fuerunt, et est, et erit (see Veszely, Imets és Kovács, op. cit., p. 67).

Chapter 5

The Romanian Gospel Book From Kalocsa

We will briefly analyze a Romanian Catholic printed text dating from the eighteenth century, which appeared in Hungary and was also used in the churches in Moldavia.

In 1796, the Piarist priest David Biró,[1] who knew Romanian, printed in Kalocsa a Gospel book with Latin letters (*Evangelie la toate duminecs si szerbetori peszte tot anul*), which included the Romanian versions of the Gospels that were read in church according to the

---

[1](Editor's Note) David Biró (1715-1773) had worked for 22 years for the Bibici family (see note 3) and was a preacher of the Romanian Catholic community in Sântana. For more details concerning the Piarists, see Ioan Iozsa-Iozsa, Piariştii şi românii până la 1918, Aiud, 1940; Alexandru Tonk, "Formarea intelectualităţii romāne din Transilvania şi liceul piariştilor din Cluj," in *Studia Universitatis Babeş-Bolyai, seria Historia*, XIII, 1968, fasc. 1, pp. 45-48. The Gospel was described for the first time by Ioan Papiu, with quotes from the original text, "Adaus de notiţe bibliografice din secolul XVII şi XVIII," in *Transilvania*, XIV, 1883, nr. 11-12, 1-15 iunie, pp. 86-89 (signed: Aenobarbu).

prescriptions of the Roman Catholic rites of those times.[2] Although the title page says that he "translated (the text), prompted by the most honourable Counselor Margareta Tomeian,"[3] it appears that the author used older Romanian translations, transcribing the texts using Latin letters and Magyar orthography, so that they could also be used by the priests who did not know Romanian well.

We should mention here that the author does not give any indication as to for whom this printed text was intended, to whom it was addressed, and what needs it answered. The only thing we know for certain is that it was addressed to Catholic believers who spoke Romanian. But who were they? Could they have been the Romanian Catholics in the Szeckler region, who were undergoing a process of Szecklerization and did not yet know Hungarian well? Could they have been the Catholics in Moldavia, who, as we know, spoke Romanian? Could they have been another group of Transylvanian Romanians converted to Catholicism?[4] At any rate, the printing of this Gospel book was not done only for the "spiritual joy" of Margareta

---

[2] See the description in Ioan Bianu and Nerva Hodoş, *Bibliografia românească veche*, vol II, pp. 191-192. The second edition appeared in Buda, in 1970 (see ibidem, p. 413).

[3] (Editor's Note) Margareta Tomeian was the wife of Iacob Bibici (?-1754), royal counsellor and vice-governor of the country of Arad, owner of the Comlăuş estate (Sântana, in the county of Arad), where he built a church and a monastery and founded a gymnasium, run by Piarist monks (1751-1790). For more details about the activities of the Piarists in Sântana and their Romanian character, see Ian Iozsa-Iozsa, op. cit., pp. 78-83.

[4] (Editor's Note) The appearance of this book is related to the activities of the Piarists in Sîntana, activities initiated by Iacob Bibici and his wife, who spoke Romanian within their family. Most of the old Catholic communities in the areas of Oaş, Hunedoara, and Banat had disappeared because they lacked Romanian priests and ministers (the communities in Bărăbanţ and Slatina-Timiş, still extant, are certified in the eighteenth century; see C. Economu, "Panegiricul din Bărăbanţ," in *Limbă şi literature*, XI, 1966, pp. 539-541; Petru Bancea, "Influenţa catolică la românii din Slatina Timişului," in *Luceafărul*, VI, 1940, nr. 7, iulie, pp. 17-22).

Tomeian, as is mentioned on the title page, but for the spiritual benefit of certain Romanian Catholics, whoever they might have been. The book also answered the pastoral needs of the priests, who, according to the ecclesiastical regulations, were obliged to read and comment on the Gospel on Sunday or on a holiday in the language of the people (*lingua vernacular*).

Before the Gospel, *praefatincula ad lectionem Evanghelii* was read, a short introduction: *Evanghelia pe astezi renduite... care spre limba romeneaske aşa s-au telmeciuit* ("The Gospel for today... which was this way translated into Romanian"), followed by the text and the sermon.

For practical reasons, at the end of the book the author added the questions that the priest addressed to the godparents during baptism and to the bride and bridegroom during the wedding ceremony.

There is no information about any Catholic Magyar Szeckler communities using the Romanian language in churches in Transylvania during the eighteenth century. Therefore, it means that the beneficiaries of the Gospel book from Kalocsa used it until sometime around the middle of the nineteenth century.[5]

The circulation of this Gospel book in Moldavia is further proof that use of the Romanian language was necessary among the Catholic believers in that country.

---

[5]A copy of the edition from 1769 was discovered in the library of the Catholic parish of Bârgăuani (in the county of Neamţ), in 1962. From the note written on the cover, it results that the book belonged to the missionary Iosif Clementis, a native of Transylvania, who in 1850 was rector in Răchiteni (in the county of Iaşi). (Editor's Note: A copy of a Cyrillic text, taken from the library of the historian Ioan Ferenţ, is being preserved at the Catholic parish in Butea (in the county of Iaşi). The manuscript proves once again that this Romanian Gospel was needed in Moldavia).

Chapter 6

The Origin and Meaning
of the Word Chango

In the Romanian language, the word *ceangău* does not mean anything, which clearly indicates that it is not of Romanian origin. In Hungarian scholarly literature, the origin and meaning of this word has given rise to numerous interpretations and hypothesis. Today it is generally accepted that the word is of Szeckler origin and that initially it had a pejorative sense. Nicolae Iorga's theory,[1] according to which the word *ceangău* is cognate with *şuvăgău, şavgău, şangău* (Hungarian *savágó*, meaning "salt cutter"), is not plausible.[2] Apart from other problems it poses, this etymology does not explain why the Changos reject this name. This is an indication that this name initially had a depreciatory sense and was attributed to them by outsiders.

---

[1] Nicolae Iorga, *Privilegiile şangăilor de la Târgu Ocna*, p. 247; *Istoria armatei româneşti*, I, Vălenii de Munte, 1910, p. 78.

[2] (Editor's Note) The etymology was taken over by August Scriban, *Dicţionarul limbii româneşti*, Iaşi, 1939, s.v. şalgău.

Living side by side with the Changos for a long time, the Szecklers knew that they were of Romanian origin. After the Changos adopted the Catholic religion during the process of Szecklerization, the Szecklers recognized them as Magyars, but did not consider them pure, authentic Magyars, but rather pseudo-Magyars. To mark the difference between themselves and the Changos, who spoke broken Hungarian, spoke Romanian at home, and had Romanian costumes and traditions, the Szecklers gave them the name of *csángó-magyarok*, which means hybrid Magyars, who speak a mixed, deteriorated Magyar language.

In the opinion of the Hungarian linguist Bernat Munkacsi, the origin of the term must be sought in the Szeckler verb *csángani* (to interbreed, in a biological sense).[3] Their name is, thus, a result of their broken, mixed Hungarian dialect. Indeed, the Hungarian dialect of the Changos is composed of Magyar elements (the vocabulary and the grammar) and Romanian elements (the pronunciation and the phonetical system). Their faulty pronunciation had been noticed by Petru Zöld, in 1766. It could not have been otherwise, as it was a Romanian pronunciation, corresponding to the Romanian basis of articulation of the speakers.

Another Magyar author, Aladár Ballagi, sees the problem in the same way: *Ce peuple s'appelle czángo, nom qui tire son origine du verbe csángani et veut dire hongrois dégénéré* ("These people are called Changos, a name which has its origin in the verb *csángani* and means degenerate Hungarians").[4]

Therefore, the origin of the name "Chango" is the following:

---

[3]Bernát Munkácsi, "A moldvai csángók nyelvjárása" ("The Dialect of the Changos in Moldavia"), in *Magyar nyelvór*, IX, 1880, p. 445.

[4]"Les Hongrois en Moldavie," in *Societatea Geografică Română. Buletin,* IX, 1888, p. 215.

csángani "to interbreed" (a biological sense);

csángó beszéd "mixed language" (a linguistic sense);

csángó-magyar "hybrid Magyar," which means one who speaks a mixed language.

Initially, the Changos represented that group of Szecklerized Romanians who spoke a hybrid, mixed, broken Hungarian dialect. Rather than accepting that they were Szecklerized Wallachians, Hungarian authors preferred the hypothesis that the Changos are degenerate Magyars. This theory conferred upon them implicitly the right, and even the duty, to bring the Changos back into the midst of the Magyar nation.

While the Magyar scholars Bernáat Munkácsi and Aladár Ballagi offered the best etymological and semantic interpretation of the name "Chango", on the other hand they avoided any kind of explanation regarding the causes that might have determined the Changos, who according to them were Magyars, and therefore members of the dominant nation, to corrupt their own language and then adopt the Wallachian language, costume, and traditions. It is clear, however, that the so-called "degenerate Magyars" were not Magyars at all, but Szecklerized Romanians who, being unable to acquire the sounds and the correct pronunciation of the Hungarian language, substituted them with sounds and phonetical elements from their native language, Romanian. The result is that the Chango Hungarian dialect has a non-Magyar phonetical system, of Romanian origin.

While for scholars in the past the Changos appeared to be degenerate Magyars, linguistic scholarship today has demonstrated that the phonetical system of the Hungarian dialect spoken by a minority among them is proof of their Romanian origin.[5] Although

---

[5]See appendix.

they had learned the language of the Szecklers, which they pronounced in their own manner, at home they continued to speak their old Romanian dialect and would not give up their Romanian individuality. Therefore, the name of Changos, namely hybrids, is a clear indication of their Romanian origin.

Although today this name is not generally accepted by those who are called by it, nevertheless it reveals their Romanian origin and the firmness with which they have preserved the language of their ancestors in difficult historical conditions that would be hard to understand in our times. It is not surprising that, after they had settled in Moldavia, their first impulse was to give up the Magyar language, which no longer held political significance, and continue to speak their old Romanian dialect, brought from Transylvania.

In a more recent period, with great material sacrifices, the Romanian state founded schools with Magyar as teaching language in a few villages in the county of Bacău, with Hungarian textbooks and Szecklers teachers brought from the other side of the mountains, to educate the Changos, allegedly, in their own language. This was a decisive conscience test concerning the origins of this population. The people thanked the authorities for the solicitude shown toward them, but continued to send their children to the schools with Romanian as the language of instruction.[6] The choice of the population confirmed its Romanian belonging.

---

[6](Editor's Note) D. Mărtinaş wrote down a few notes about these schools, relating information he had received from Mihai Gherguţă in Bacău: "The Romanian people did not enjoy and did not become attached to the Hungarian system of education. They did not send their children to Hungarian schools, which, after a difficult period of two or three years, had to be closed down for lack of pupils. The founding of these schools was only experimental. The test failed completely..." (*Caiet nenumerotat*, 1967, p. 140). As one who belonged to this community and as a scholar, Mihai Gherguţă stated: "The period when it was compulsory to learn Hungarian was a disaster for pupils, for their parents, and for school in general" (letter to V.M.U., dated 10

Compelled by necessity, we have used, in the present study, the name of *Changos* when referring to this population. The reason is that it has become a commonly accepted term in scholarship to refer to this population which has had a unique historical development, but cannot be considered a separate ethnic group. Nevertheless, a better term for them would be Romanian Catholics.

Objectively speaking, the Changos are right when they do not accept this name. In their great majority, they no longer even speak broken Hungarian, as they abandoned this language during the first half of the nineteenth century. They are neither degenerate Magyars, nor Hungarians Romanianized by the Moldavians, but Romanians who went through a process of Szecklerization, who, after settling in Moldavia, abandoned the Hungarian language, which they had only recently acquired for social and political reasons, and continued to speak, to this day, Romanian in their specific Transylvanian dialect.

November 1982). To put an end to this disaster he submitted a memo to the Central Committee of the Ploughmen's Front, where he demanded that "these schools should be closed down and that young people should be allowed to learn as their parents and grandparents had, i.e., in Romanian." See, for example, notes 84 and 94.

Chapter 7

Controversies among Italian and Hungarian Missionaries

The information regarding the precarious situation of the Magyar language in the villages of Moldavia alarmed the Bishop of Alba Iulia, Ignaţiu Batthyáni. On 6 October 1787, he addressed Pope Pius VI, expressing his sorrow for the sad fate of the Magyar believers in Moldavia, who, he said, did not understand any other language but Hungarian. Not knowing this language, the Italian missionaries could not preach and catechize in the language of the people. Therefore, the pastoring was being done in unsatisfactory conditions, thus endangering the spiritual life of the believers and causing damage to the Church. In the end, the bishop indicated the solution: the pope should order that the Italians be withdrawn from the mission and replaced by Magyar missionaries sent by him.

The petition of the bishop of Alba Iulia is understandable with regard to the few villages of bilingual Changos of the southern group and the few villages of Szecklers on the valley of the Trotuş, although in these villages the population understood Romanian as well. But the petition was unfounded where the great majority of the villages in the basin of the Siret were concerned, especially those in the northern group, where the population had given up the Hungarian language altogether and spoke only Romanian. Well-informed on the realities in

Moldavia, the pope replied to the bishop on 7 January 1788, making it very clear that the situation was not so alarming and, therefore, there was no reason for him to be sorrowful. The Italian missionaries used the Romanian language as that was the native language of the majority of the Catholic population in the region. For satisfying the spiritual needs of the believers who spoke the Hungarian language, the primate cardinal of Esztergom was authorized to send two missionaries who spoke this language to Moldavia.[1]

The Magyar missionaries argued that the greatest part of the Transylvanian Changos, at that time recently established in Moldavia, were bilingual or, at least, understood the Magyar language, as well, and, therefore, forgotten, and so that all Catholic believers would be pastored in the Hungarian language and only by Hungarian priests. It is not difficult to understand the political motive behind these actions, that of continuing in Moldavia the linguistic Magyarization initiated in the Szeckler region. The main obstacle to this plan was not coming from the Italian missionaries but from somewhere else, and it could not be easily eliminated. What worried the Hungarian church authorities was that the Changos were indifferent or even hostile to the

---

[1]Domokos Pál Péter, op. cit., p. 61 (Editor's Note: Batthyáni had also claimed the title of apostolic dean of Moldavia. See also N. Iorga, *Studii şi documente*, I-II, pp. 138-139; Pietro Tocanel, op. cit., pp. 20-21. Rome knew well the real situation in Moldavia from previous documents. Thus, in the note sent to the Fide Propaganda in 1745, it is stated that: "The language whose knowledge is absolutely necessary so that the missionary priests be understood is the Wallachian or Moldavian language." The sender warned that the arrival of Hungarian priests in Moldavia would plant seed of scandal (un seminario di scandali), because of the misunderstandings and conflicts that would follow (the future would bear this our fully). "The congregation would enjoy no peace, and the Magyar priests, since they would not speak Moldavian, could not fully officiate as missionaries, for there would be no need for the Hungarian language here. For the benefit of the people, as well as of the mission, it is necessary that a Wallachian or Moldavian lecturer be appointed at the apostolic college in Assisi" (see G. Călinescu, *Alcuni Missionari*, p. 184).

Hungarian language which they had recently given up. This language was hard to learn and pronounce, while Romanian was their mother tongue which they had been speaking for centuries. The Italian missionaries did not cooperate in any way with the propagation of the Magyar language, as they preferred the Romanian language, which was much more accessible to them: *un linguaggio facilissimo*, a fact also recognized by their adversaries. The reader must not think that the recalcitrant attitude of the population was dictated by some sort of xenophobe tendencies. If the Changos opposed the Hungarian language, their gesture was spontaneous, unpremeditated, and was simply the expression of their Romanian linguistic tradition. The people spoke the way their heart and nature dictated, the way it was easier for them. Even though they were able, occasionally, to speak Hungarian, their usual, everyday language was Romanian, their native language.

The supreme ecclesiastical authority intervened in this thorny problem and solved it, taking into consideration the objective situation. What is of interest to historians is the fact that, already in 1788, the Roman Curia knew that the native language of the great majority of the Catholic population in Moldavia was Romanian and gave its approval that this language be used in pastoring. But what determined the victory of the Romanian language in this controversy was the firm attitude of the population. Despite what the church authorities in Alba Iulia or Rome might have believed, despite what the scholars of the time believed regarding their language and nationality, despite the fact that often even the Romanian authorities, misinformed, saw these inhabitants as a Hungarian population, they continued, then as today, to speak in their traditional Romanian language. Even though this population, in general, was not educated in those times, even though its national consciousness was still in an embryonic state, even if they lacked educated leaders to enlighten them,[2] these people possessed a powerful and clear consciousness of their tradition and their Romanian linguistic belonging.

Noi asă grăim cum am primit gi la oamini sîi vek, alfeli nu scim sî grăim, nu pucem. Asă-i la noi. Unguresci nu scim sî grăim. Nu pucem. Unguri îs altî limbî gi oamin ("We speak the way we learned from the old ones, we do not know how to speak in any other way, we cannot. This is how we are. We do not know how to speak Hungarian. We cannot. Hungarian is the language of a different people"); this is what old Mariţa Ladan (85 years old), from Butea (in the county of Iaşi), explained to us in 1960.

For the Hungarian missionaries, the bilingualism of the Changos, a result of their Szecklerization, which today has disappeared almost entirely, was the pretext that they would permanently set forth to support the thesis that these were Magyars and therefore they had to be pastored in the Hungarian language. The discussions around this problem caused endless controversies between the Italian missionaries, who represented almost the entire Catholic clergy in Moldavia, and the few Magyar missionaries, causing problems for the pope's Chancellery and the Hapsburg Chancellery, because of their frequent

---

[2]The only leaders were the missionary priests, most of them Italian. The merit of having understood their natural inclination for the Romanian language rests with Italian missionaries, who used it despite all the invectives and pressures coming from their adversaries. The missionaries' parish had a practical character, which entered deeply into the population's consciousness: they were not only confessors, but also judges and guides in the most varied aspects of life. From the missionaries, this social role later passed to the priests raised from among them (for further reference see: Constantin C. Diculescu, *Din corespondenţele episcopului Melchisedec*, Bucureşti, 1909, p. 36; Moţu, *Politica noastră future*, Bucureşti, f.a., p. 134). Compared with the possibilities, the results were good. Earl d'Hauterive wrote about the Catholics in Moldavia in 1787: *Aussi sont-ils plus actifs, plus aisés et plus stables* (so they are not "wanderers" or "rolling stones" as some have interpreted the term Chango). See *Memoriu asupra vechei şi actualei stări a Moldovei*, p. 88.

complaints. The Magyar missionaries used every means to try to attract adherents, bringing psalm readers from the Szeckler region. The Szeckler psalm readers often proved themselves to be propagators of the Magyar language, catechizing the youth in the church and teaching the people to sing and pray in Hungarian, "so that God would listen to their prayers."[3]

The Magyar missionaries understood Catholicism only within the framework and under the shield of the Hungarian language, arguing that the Romanian language was dangerous for the Catholic faith. The people, however, wished to live their religious life according to their old customs and in the Romanian language. This process of Szecklerization was successful in some villages of the southern group, but in the great majority of villages it could not replace the linguistic consciousness of the population, who continued to speak and pray in Romanian.

Disappointed and refusing to admit openly that their efforts to Szecklerize the Changos outside the Magyar borders had failed, the

---

[3](Editor's Note) Bringing Szeckler church singers from Transylvania had an economic motive behind it: since he was not native, the church singer was exempted from tribute, which was to be paid by the Romanian community. For more details about the Szeckler singer from Săbăoani, see the account by Miron Pompiliu, published by N. Bănescu, "O 'misiune' a lui Miron Pompiliu," in *Convorbiri literare*, XLIII, 1909, nr. 12, dec., p. 1303 (Miron Pompiliu had been sent in Moldavia by George Bariţiu, on the trail of the Society "Saint Ladislau" deputation in Pesta, which had come to Romania with a plan aimed to restore the old Hungarian kingdom; see the resumé of the letters sent by the bishops Pluym and Salandari to Cardinal Barnabo, and published by I. Dumitriu-Snagov in *Le Saint-Siége et la Roumanie moderne 1866-1877. Régestes...*, Rome, 1984). In 1933, the priest Iosif Ghiuzan's grandfather, aged 90, died at Adjudeni; he remembered the church singer Fechete, who had come to Ditrău, who sang in Hungarian in church without being understood by the people (Iosif Gabor, *Ierarhia catolică a Moldovei*, II, p. 229, note 451, in manuscript). "In 1947, Veronica Erdeş (aged 80) from Butea told me that as a child she had been taught by a Szeckler church singer to pray in Hungarian: *Az Ocianok es Fiunok es Sentlelek.* Amen. When her mother heard her, she admonished her" (D. Mărtinaş).

Magyar missionaries accused the Italian missionaries that, instead of devoting themselves to their religious mission, they occupied themselves with the Romanianization of the Changos.[4] As if the Italian missionaries, who spoke only broken Romanian, would have been able to Romanianize them. Later on, the Magyar publicists would accuse the Moldavians of denationalizing and assimilating the "poor Magyar Changos." As if the Moldavians could have had anything to do with the fact that the Changos were speaking Romanian in their old Transylvanian dialect. Both accusations were unfair, but they had a great impact on Hungarian public opinion and on Hungarian scholarship in the past.

The rapid regression of the Hungarian language among the Changos at the end of the eighteenth and the beginning of the nineteenth century has, however, another explanation. In the conditions of the past, in the Szeckler region, the Hungarian language, adopted during the process of Szecklerization, had proven its utility as a connecting bridge between the Changos and the dominant nation. Outside the Szeckler region, in Moldavia, it was no longer of use to anyone. The Changos communicated very well with the Moldavians in Romanian. In church, the priests also spoke Romanian. Losing its social and political function, the Hungarian language lost the importance it had had before the Changos emigrated from

---

[4]See the account given by Iosif Tomassi in I. Dumitru Snagov, *op. cit.,* pp. 376-377. One of the most scheming Magyar missionaries, an adventurer striving to become a bishop in Moldavia, was Ştefan Bocskor, who perturbed the peace within the mission between 1799-1815. In order to attain his ends, this *povero pazzo*, as the nuncio in Vienna called him, had no scruples: inciting the population, substitutions of persons (in 1804, he sent his brother to Rome, together with three young Hungarians from Transylvania, who pretended to be envoys from Moldavia), complaints at the nunciature of Vienna, fake letters sent to Rome, including forgeries of public papers (passports and decrees of the Congregation for Fide Propaganda), for which he was arrested and then sentenced by canonical trial. For more details see Pietro Tocanel, *op. cit.,* pp. 53-93).

Transsylvania. As a result, during the first decades of the nineteenth century, this language disappeared from most of the Catholic communities. It was maintained only in a few villages, almost all of them in the southern group, whose inhabitants had gone through a longer and more profound process of Szecklerization. In the great majority of the village bilingualism ceased to exist.

The Italian missionaries, alien to any intentions of Magyarization, saw no danger in the Romanian language. The Catholic population, in its great majority, whenever it had a free choice, outside any constraints, chose to speak its native language, Romanian. Moreover, one should not forget that, besides the Changos (Transylvanian Romanians), there were also some native Moldavians who were of Catholic religion.

Regarding the problem of pastoring, the Italian bishops and priests were consistently on the side of the Romanian language, due to the objective situation, and also because of the natural inclination that they felt for the Romance language of their parishioners.

The fact that the Hungarian missionaries fought with every means at their disposal to determine the Changos to speak Hungarian was due to a grave misconception on their part. Like the Hungarian scholars of those times, they did not understand that the Changos did not speak the Moldavian dialect, but that they spoke Romanian in their Transylvanian dialect, which they had learned neither from the Moldavians nor from the Italian missionaries. These missionaries, who did not know Romanian, could not discern between these two dialects. The Changos spoke Romanian because they were Transylvanian Romanians. If some of them were bilingual, also speaking broken Hungarian, that was the result of the policy of Magyarization in Transylvania. In the conditions of their escape from the estates of their feudal lords in Transylvania and from under the oppression of

Hungarian domination, the attempt of the missionaries to bring them back to the Magyar language and nation was doomed to fail.

Chapter 8

The Szecklerization of the Romanians and the Origins of the Chango Phenomenon

*All things are better understood if they are told
from their beginning.*

—   - Miron Costin

Let us try to penetrate deeper into the mystery of the origin of the Chango phenomenon to understand it better, as the chronicler says. The problem we wish to discuss is the following: is there any connection between the origin of this phenomenon and the process of Szecklerization of the Romanians in Transylvania?

The answer to this question requires knowledge of the history of the Romanians in the Szeckler region. Unfortunately, this dramatic history was very little known to the historians of the past. Nowadays, the history of the Romanians in the Szeckler region has been studied better and there is no need for new evidence to demonstrate that the villages in southeastern Transylvania were subjected to a long process of linguistic Szecklerization in the past, with the result that the demographic situation was radically changed in favor of the dominant nation. The numerical proportion of the Szecklers increased considerably, while the number of Romanians decreased.

Another result of the process of Szecklerization was the appearance of the Changos in the Szeckler region, a phenomenon which Hungarian scholars passed over in silence. The interest of the Hungarian authorities was to conceal the Romanian origin of the Changos, so that everyone would consider them pure Hungarians. Neglected by everyone, the real origin of the Chango phenomenon began to be forgotten, scholars adopting an attitude like that of Domokos Pál Péter: "It is difficult to provide an answer to the questions: who are the Changos in Moldavia? When did they establish themselves in the regions in which they live today? Who Christianized them in the Catholic religion and when? And who taught them to speak Hungarian?"

Unfortunately, the author neglected to ask a few more questions, which, in themselves, suggested an answer: why do they wear Romanian costumes? Why do they have Romanian customs and follow way of life similar to that of the Romanians? Why do most of them have Romanian names? Why does their great majority speak Romanian in a Transylvanians dialect? And how does one explain the resemblances between the Changos and the Romanians of Transylvania?

The process of Szecklerization took place slowly, over a long period of time. It began in the fourteenth and fifteenth centuries and continued into the twentieth century. It goes without saying that this process could not have been uniform throughout the whole Szeckler region. It varied in intensity and in relation to the local conditions and the proximity of the centers of Szecklers influence. Romanian villages that were located near the administrative, cultural, and ecclesiastical centers frequently came into contact with the Szecklers, were assimilated faster, and acquired a dialect closer to that of the

Szecklers. Villages in the outlying areas, in the mountains,[1] having few contacts with the Szecklers, acquired a more corrupted Szeckler dialect. The Romanians heard the Hungarian sounds in their own way and reproduced them according to their manner of pronunciation, to their own basis of hearing and articulation. In such villages a distinctive Hungarian idiom developed, with its own phonetical system, different from the traditional phonetical system of the Magyar language. The Szecklers recognized that it was a corrupted dialect of Hungarian and called it *csángó beszéd*, meaning hybrid language. Zöld confirmed this name, showing that the Changos spoke Hungarian *multo blesius* (*sehr unangenehm*), in a very lisping, unpleasant way. After they had settled in Moldavia, where they were no longer in close contact with the Szecklers, they remained irrevocably with this variant of the Hungarian dialect. Weigand's finding, related by Rubinyi, is very significant in this respect, namely that they spoke Hungarian like children who tried to pronounce the sounds of the language.[2] The cause of this strange pronunciation was not the presumed Cuman origin of the speakers, but their Romanian basis of articulation.

Initially, the name of Changos was attributed to those Szecklerized Romanians[3] who developed a corrupted Hungarian

---

[1](Editor's Note) "Most Wallachians live in the most mountainous regions, in those places which the conquerors have left behind them," remarks Baron Kemény Gábor, *Nagy-Enyednek és vidékének veszedelme 1848-1889-ben*, Pest, 1863, p. 25.

[2]Rubinyi Mózes, "Ujabb adalékok a csángók nyelvjárásához" ("New Contributions Regarding the Dialect of the Changos"), in *Magyar nyelvöl*, 1902, p. 3. See also Veress Endre, op. cit., p. 5.

[3](Editor's Note) "Our Romanians living among the Szecklers at the edge of Ciuc and Trei Scaune have been called Changos so far, not Szecklers, a fact which reveals their foreign origin" (Sabin Opreanu, "Printre românii săcuizaţi," in *Graiul românesc*, I, 1927, nr. 1, ian., p. 11). The term is toponimically certified as well: Ciangăi, the old name for the village of Cărpineni, the commune of Poiana, in the county of Covasna (see Ion Iordan, Petre Gâştescu, D.I. Oancea, *Indicatorul localităţilor din România*, Bucureşti, 1974, p. 106).

dialect, with a distinctive phonetical system, different from the Magyar-Szeckler one. At home, these Romanians preferred to speak Romanian, while in their relations with the Szecklers, with the priests, and with the administrative authorities, they used their newly adopted dialect, which, however, they pronounced differently from their interlocutors. From the name given by them to this dialect, which they called *csángó beszéd* (hybrid language), the Szecklers began calling the ones who spoke it *csángók*, Changos, namely hybrids. Some called them *csángó-magyarok*, meaning Hungarian Changos, considering them a peripheral, degenerate category of Hungarians, mixed with Romanians, from whom they had adopted their language, costume, and customs. From their perspective, the Szecklerized Romanians had become hybrid Hungarians, Changos. This name, ironic at first, eventually changed its pejorative meaning[4], as political circumstances dictated. Later on, the Changos were considered to be pure Hungarians, descendants of their ancestors from Atelkuz, who, for a millennium, had managed to remain intact, living in the valleys of the Siret, the Moldova, and the Bistriţa rivers. Consequently, Romantic nationalists began to claim that they belonged to the Magyar nation, and considered that the territory on which they lived was Magyar land.

However, this theory was very far from the historical facts. The Changos did not consider themselves Hungarians, they lived according to their Romanian traditions and, as many scholars noted, spoke a specifically Transylvanian Romanian dialect, an expression of their

---

[4](Editor's Note) It's pejorative meaning was changed with regard to those who created the term. Bálint Csüry states that in Hungarian, the denomination of Changos has a collective character, extending to all the Hungarians living abroad or in southeastern Transylvania, while admitting that at the beginning this name was subject to ridicule. The Changos in Moldavia, whose origin could not be established, consider it as such even today (see "Egy és más a moldavai csángók nyelvéről" – "Observations on the Language of the Changos in Moldavia," in *Pasztotuz*, Cluj, XXI, 1935, no. 5-7, 15 March-15 April, pp. 140-141).

Romanian origin. These scholars, however, failed to notice the scholarly error that they had fallen into, and explained this fact as a result of their denationalization and linguistic assimilation by the Moldavian Romanians.

The problem of the Romanians in the Szeckler region, which remained almost unknown for a long time, was carefully studied during the interwar period, through the efforts of some Transylvanian scholars, among them we mention G. Popa-Lisseanu, Sabin Opreanu, Ştefan Manciulea, Teodor Chindea, and others.

Before the process of Szecklerization began, before their religious and linguistic metamorphosis, the history of the ancestors of those people called Changos was one and the same with the history of the Romanian serfs. The Changos do not represent a nation of enigmatic people of unknown origin, coming from somewhere in the East, as some historians and journalists of the past have suggested. They appeared in the demographic landscape of southeastern Transylvania, with their specific character, with their Romanian-Hungarian bilingualism, and with a corrupted Hungarian dialect, as a result of the process of Szecklerization of the Romanian villages in that region. Outside of this territory and these historical conditions, they could not be identified, despite the arduous research of many scholars.[5]

---

[5](Editor's Note) The few Changos in Hunedoara and the Banat were brought here from Bucovina, beginning in 1880 (see Dr. Victor Şuiaga, "Ciangăii din Hunedoara, Cristur şi Streisângeorgiu," ibidem, nr. 24, 3 aug., p. 3; Silviu Dragomir, "Vechimea elementului românesc şi colonizările streine în Banat," in *Anuarul Institutului de Istorie Naţională, Cluj*, III, 1924, p. 291). The Lutheran Changos from Săcele (Braşov) belong to the same area of southeastern Transylvania (for more details about them see Kolumbán Lajos, A hétfalusi csángok a multban és jelenben – Ceangăii din Săcele Braşovului. *Contribuţii istorice documentare la vechimea elementului românesc in Ţara Bârsei, Satulung-Săcele*, 1937; Liviu Marcu, "Vechi obiceiuri juridice în subzone Săcele (a doua jumătate a secolului XIX-prima jumătate a secolului XX)," in *Cumidava*, V, 1971, pp. 569-606). Here is a quote from Kolumbán's work Portul (The Costume) about the Changos' Romanian

The process of Szecklerization of the Romanians is not tied to a certain historical moment; it was determined by local circumstances, initially by integration into one of the received religions (Catholic or Protestant) of a group of families, of a village, sometimes of a group of villages, a slow but continuous process, which lasted until the twentieth century. The poor organization of the Romanian Church, the lack of priests, and the poverty of the serf villages were the causes that led many Romanians to abandon their religious community and convert to the well-organized and wealthy churches of the Szecklers. In the absence of a Romanian priest, the population appealed to the Szeckler priests for different religious services (baptisms, weddings, funerals), which eventually led to the permanent joining of the people to the religion in which they had been baptized or married. The necessities of life, the pressure from the environment and from the political and administrative system, the mixed marriages, the

---

characteristics: "The long shirt and the belt make a Chango look like an authentic Vlach" (p. 33). "Indeed, if a foreigner sees a Chango dressed like this, he will think that he is a Vlach. The Magyar does not acknowledge him as his Hungarian brother" (p. 25). This characteristic also applies to the Szecklers: "a hundred years ago, a Chango's clothes were more or less the same with those of a Vlach's, and thus if a Szeckler looked at a Chango, he would not acknowledge him as his Hungarian brother" (p. 35). Limba (The Language): "The Changos use many Wallachian words, and if they do not want to speak correctly about a certain thing, they use (and they still do) Wallachian words instead of Hungarian ones" (p. 24). Dansul (The Dance): "As far as their dances are concerned, the national Hungarian characteristics have been lost. Until 40 years ago, at Satulung, both the Chango and the Vlach had known no other dances than the Wallachian ones, first of all, hora (the Romanian ring dance), which proves the Dacian-Roman idea, and also brâul, and purtata" (p. 24). "If the young Chango people wanted to party, they had to ask for the priest's permission, not the administrator's [in Moldavia, too, this custom has been practiced until nowadays, the author's emphasis], then the party would take place not at the rhythm of a passionate czardas, but at a monotonous Wallachian tune" (p. 81). Obiceiuri româneşti (see pp. 72, 95, 105-108). Of course, all these aspects are not devoid of significance and they are not the result of any Romanian influence, as the author believes, but they represent essential elements demonstrating their Romanian origin.

proselytism of the Szeckler clergy, and the absence, to a great extent, of Romanian priests, all determined the Romanians in this region to turn to one of the official religions, especially the Catholic one, which remained strong in this region despite the triumph of the Reformation in the rest of Transylvania.

Under the old Hungarian kingdom, the process of Magyarization began early and continued during the existence of the Transylvanian principality, through the assimilation of the Romanian ruling class, the *cnezi*, the boyars, and the voievods, which resulted in their inclusion in the Magyar nobility. This process extended to the Romanian villages in the Szeckler region, in which, after the conclusion of the alliance of the three privileged nations (*Unio trium nationum*, 1438) the political and social-economic situation of the serfs worsened. The Szeckler nobles deprived the Romanians of any liberties and rights, of any leaders and schools. As a result of this situation, and of the promises made to them, numerous Romanian villages began to orientate themselves toward the official churches of the Szecklers, whose members enjoyed incomparably superior political, economic, and cultural privileges. The deplorable economic situation to which the Romanian serfs had been reduced following the Verboczian legislation and the cruel treatment they received from the ruling classes was noted by Emperor Joseph II, who was not exaggerating when, on the occasion of his trip to Transylvania in 1773, horrified by what he saw, reported the following to his mother, Hapsburg Empress Maria Theresa: "These poor Romanian subjects, who, undoubtedly, are the older and more numerous inhabitants of Transylvania, are being crushed under the burden of injustices and maltreated by everyone, by the Magyars, as well as by the Saxons, to such an extent that their fate, when you know it, arouses your pity, and it is surprising that there are still so many of these people and that they have not all fled."[6] This refers to the mass flight of the Transylvanian peasants to the two Romanian principalities.

Bishop Ioan Inocentie Micu-Clain, the defender of the rights of the Romanians, overwhelmed with grief, showed in one of the memorable meetings of the Diet that the Romanian serfs "are oppressed till blood is drawn" and that "besides their own skin, nothing else is left for them to eat... and sometimes even their skin is flayed."[7] That was the harsh reality of those times. But these grievances were not addressed. The society of that time was so differentiated by class and the fate of the Romanian serfs was so terrible that even a representative of the Magyar ruling class, Baron Wesselenyi, his own consciousness being offended, admitted with lucidity: "The three nations and the four received religions constitute the seven deadly sins of Transylvania."

In this drastic situation, the serfs had no perspective of salvation. A solution had to be found and it could only be adaptation or escape

---

[6]See the German text in I. Lupaş, *Împăratul Iosif II şi răscoala ţăranilor din Transilvania*, Bucureşti, 1935, p. 8. (Editor's Note: See also C. Sassu, *Românii şi ungurii*, Bucureşti, 1940, pp. 119-120. The wretched situation confronting the Romanians in Transylvania is also described by the botanist Bathasar Hacquet (1739-1815), who witnessed it: "This neglected and oppressed nation sways over the worst land in the entire country. they are deprived of these lands as soon as they have cleared them by the sweat of their brow and when they are about to sow maize. Each Szeckler or Hungarian can appropriate a Romanian's land, even if the latter has been its master for hundreds of years. The Romanian is driven away to the mountains together with this whole family and all he can find there is rocks, and sometimes he is forced to leave the country" (see Victor Jinga, *Problemele fundamentale ale Transilvaniei*, II, Braşov, 1945, p. 202; G. Bogdan-Duică, "Din trecutul nostru," in *Tribuna*, XI, 1894, nr. 160, 30 iul./11 aug., pp. 1-2). See also Ioan Pop, "Relatări privind stările de fapt din Transilvania în timpul vizitei lui Iosif al doilea (1773)," in *Marisia*, VII, 1977, pp. 111-124.

7Augustin Bunea, *Din istoria românilor, Episcopul Ioan Inocenţiu Klein, (1728-1751)*, Blaj, 1900, p. 99.

across the border. Under these circumstances, it is not difficult to understand why hundreds of Romanian villages in the Szeckler region gradually became converted to the official religions, becoming in time Szeckler villages, increasing the numbers of Szecklers. To be able to survive biologically, they were condemned to die as a nation. While the conversion to one of the received religions was tied to the hope for an amelioration of their social and economic condition, it also coincided with the beginning of the process of Szecklerization, which later became stronger and stronger and was being carried out with all the means that the ecclesiastical and civil authorities had at their disposal, with the protecting help of the feudal lords. These extremely difficult historical conditions led to the appearance of the Chango phenomenon in southeastern Transylvania, as well as the settling of the Changos in Moldavia, which was part of the massive exodus of the Transylvanian population in the eighteenth century.

* * *

Typical for the process of Szecklerization of the Romanian population is the example of the villages Vlăhiţa (*Oláhfalu*) and Breţcu (*villa valachalis Bereczk*), which were ruled by Romanian *cnezi* (Ursu, in 1301; Ioan and Radu, in 1426) and lived according to the old Romanian law (*jus valachicum*). In time, these two old Romanian settlements became Szeckler villages. The same thing happened with many other Romanian settlements which, pressured by circumstances and the environment, and hoping for more humane living conditions, converted to one of the four received religions, especially Catholicism and Calvinism, the process continuing up to the early twentieth century.[8] In the seventeenth century, the militant

---

[8](Editor's Note) The process of Magyarization also extended upon the Orthodox and Greek-Catholic Romanians, a fact which is acknowledged by Hungarian authors (see

proselytism of the Calvinist princes in Transylvania (Gavril Bethlen, Gheorghe Rákóczi II) resulted in the conversion to Calvinism of some Romanian priests and villages. This is how this phenomenon looks to historians today: a certain village, which used to be Romanian, after one or two centuries appears in documents as a village of Magyar language and religion, while it is not possible to establish the date when and the circumstances in which this metamorphosis took place.

An example of individual Magyarization is offered by the great scholar Joannes Kajoni (1629-1687). This humanist erudite, whose Romanian name was Ioan Căianu, *valachus de Kis-Kajon* (Căianu Mic), born *ex parentibus schismaticis* (of Orthodox parents), was converted to Catholicism when he was young and became a Franciscan priest. He was an enlightened and active clergyman, an organist, a renowned musician, who left us two musical anthologies: *Codex Caioni,* in which we find the first Romanian folk songs transcribed in musical notes, and *Cantionale Catholicum,* a collection of religious songs, used by the Szeckler psalm readers in the Catholic churches in Moldavia, from which many texts were later translated into Romanian, to be learned and sung by the majority of the believers.[9] He spent most of his time in the Szeckler region; he also lived in Moldavia for a while, at a monastery in Bacău. A prominent

---

Orbán Balázs, *A Székelyföld leirása – Descrierea secuimii,* I-V, Pest, 1868-1871, passim), these Romanians being also claimed by and for the Hungarian nation (for a short period of time the Greek-Catholics were included in the bishopric of Hajdúdorog, founded in 1912, see Ştefan Manciulea, "Episcopia greco-catolică maghiară de Hajdú-Dorog şi românii," in *Cultura creştină,* XXII, 1942, nr. 7-9, iul.-sept., pp.385-409 (including information on the Romanians' being made Szecklers). See Augustin Paul (Delaletca), *Între Someş şi Prut,* pp. 218-238 (chapter "Români cari nu ştiu româneşte").

[9](Editor's Note) For more details about the influence of his music in Moldavia, see Viorel Cosma, "300 de ani de la apariţia antologici de cîntece a lui Ioan Căianu," in *Musica,* 1977, nr. 1, ian., pp. 21-28).

personality that rose from among the Magyarized Romanians, who would later receive the name of Changos, Ioan Căianu "is, undoubtedly, the most expressive spiritual synthesis of feudal musical culture in Transylvania."[10] A scholar of Romanian origin and of Latin formation through Hungarian schools, he was the product of the conditions specific to the Szeckler region. The case of Căianu is similar to that of many other Romanians who distinguished themselves in the Magyar-Szeckler cultural environment, but whom history did not record or has not yet brought to light.[11]

* * *

Another important economic cause, which facilitated the process of Szecklerization, were the so-called *composesorate.*[12] These immense estates, which included vast forests, agricultural fields, and pastures, belonged to the state, but they were administered by the Szeckler communities. To benefit from the goods they produced, one had to be a member of a Szeckler community. For the Szecklers, the

---

[10]Vasile Mocanu, *Ioan Căianu,* Bucureşti, 1973, p. 5.

[11](Editor's Note) The characterization made by the author is only partially true. This *vir praeclarissimorum, talentorum, laborissimus et perpetus memoria dignus,* as he was extolled when expressing his monastic vote, later named "Petru Pázmány of Transylvania," was a Romanian scholar of humanist education who spoke both Romanian and Magyar, without being Magyarized. He asserted his Romanian origin by signing his works and the organs made in Transylvania with the name *Valachus.* (Mihai Diaconescu, "Datorie şi mărturie," in *Vatra,* XI, 1981, nr. 10, 20 oct., p. 127). See also Elisabeta Mukenhaupt, "Însemnări aparţinînd umanistului transilvănean Ioan Căianu, aflate în colecţia de carte veche a Muzeului din Miercurea Ciuc," in *Revista muzeelor şi monumentelor. Muzee,* XVI, 1979, nr. 6, p. 72, note 3.

[12]For more details about *composesorate* see G. Popa-Lisseanu, "Composesoratele secuieşti," in *Universul,* XLIX, 1932, nr. 269, 30 sept., pp. 1-2; Ioan N. Ţuţuianu, *Mijloace folosite de Ungaria pentru deznaţionalizarea românilor,* Bucureşti, 1937, pp. 75-91.

usufruct of those goods constituted a prerogative of an inestimable value and importance; for the Romanians, who had been dispossessed of their properties, it constituted a revolting inequity. The usufruct of these goods represented one of the elements of the great attraction that led the impoverished Romanian villages in Szecklerization. That was the spirit of the Verboczian legislation.

The process of Szecklerization is also reflected in the statistics of the time. There are no statistics from the fifteenth to the seventeenth centuries, although the process of Szecklerization was underway. Official data exists, however, beginning with the eighteenth century. Thus, between the years 1733 and 1760, in the counties of Odorhei, Trei Scaune, Ciuc, and Mureş, Romanians, although their numbers had declined could still be found in 372 villages. After one century, the demographic situation in these counties was the following: the Romanians had disappeared completely from 119 villages, and almost completely from another 123 villages. They remained only in 130 villages.[13] What happened with the Romanians in those 242 villages? Most of them, being in an advanced process of Szecklerization, were integrated within the Szeckler nation, and the rest emigrated to Wallachia and especially to Moldavia. among these were the Changos as well.

It goes without saying that the official statistics, according to which all the inhabitants who belonged to one of the received religions were, by definition, Magyars, must be looked upon with reservations. After their religious conversion and their statistical incorporation among the Szecklers, the Romanians continued to live for a long time according to their traditional way of life. Language, costume, and traditions are ethnic components that cannot be easily changed, neither through religious conversions, nor by statistics.

---

[13]G. Popa-Lisseanu, *Secuii şi secuizarea românilor,* Bucureşti, 1932, pp. 38-39.

The conversion to Catholicism or to another official religion, and the acquiring of the Hungarian language, represents the starting point, *terminus a quo*, which marks the appearance in the Szeckler region of the Chango phenomenon. This starting point is not the same, chronologically, for all groups of Changos. In some villages it is old, dating back to the fifteenth century as is the case of the communities in Vlăhiţa and Breţcu; in others, it is more recent. In most of the villages of the Changos who emigrated to Moldavia in the eighteenth century, Szecklerization was in its early phases, the inhabitants speaking mostly Romanian. This explains the fact that here, in the majority of the villages, the Hungarian language was quickly abandoned and completely forgotten by the population.

Szecklers, like Romanians, are good at giving nicknames. In former times, they invented another name for those who had been Szecklerized, namely that of *ot* (*tiz*) *koronas magyar*, which means "Hungarian worth five or ten crowns," because the custom was to give those who converted to one of the received religions modest financial help.[14] This name illustrates the motives driving the process of Szecklerization among the Romanians, which led to the Chango phenomenon. Living between the Romanians and the Szecklers, many Changos who remained in Transylvania were gradually absorbed by the Szecklers, losing the peculiarities of their adopted language, which became integrated, over time, in the Szeckler language. Only those established in Moldavia quickly forgot the language that they had learned in Transylvania, managing to preserve their historical identity and the continuity of their language, costume, and ancient traditions, namely their Romanian ethnic identity.

The development of the Changos cannot be looked upon as a unique phenomenon in history, without antecedents. The two

---

[14]*Ibidem*, p. 43.

languages formerly spoken by the Changos, Romanian and Hungarian, demonstrate, without any doubt, that it is not a question of an enigmatic appearance of some strangers of unknown origin, arrived from who knows where, but of a historical process that took place between the Romanians and the Szecklers, more precisely of a process of Szecklerization of the Romanians living in very unfavorable circumstances. The Romanian phonetical elements found in the Chango Hungarian dialect prove the existence of a Romanian linguistic substratum which, during this process, transmitted part of its phonetical characteristics to the adopted language.

Chapter 9

The Changos in Moldavia

In the eighteenth century, the Changos split into two groups: part of them emigrated to Moldavia, where most of them quickly forgot their adopted Hungarian tongue, but their majority remained in Transylvania where, little by little, they were absorbed almost entirely by the Szecklers, some of them still preserving their old Romanian names, today Szecklerized (*Kozokár, Kozán, Preszekár, Eszpatár, Daradics,* etc.).

The Changos established in Moldavia must not be mistaken for the descendants of the old Magyar-Szeckler colonists of this area. In addition, there is no evidence that they are descendants of the Cumans, who lived for a time in Moldavia, until the great invasion of the Tartars in 1241. The sibilant pronunciation, which Weigand thought to be of Cuman origin, has since proved to be unknown to the Cuman language.[1] Most of the Magyar-Szeckler and Saxon inhabitants of the old Moldavian Catholic communities had disappeared at the end of the eighteenth century, and the remains of these communities were now Romanian. The Changos represented a new stratification of Romanian population from Transylvania, more or less Szecklerized, and settled

---

[1] See Melich János, "A moldvai csángók eredetéhez" ("Contribution Regarding the Origin of the Changos in Moldavia"), in *Ethnographia*, Budapest, XIV, 1903, no. 1-2, January-February, pp. 52-54. See also pp. 15, 79.

here successively during the following century. Their specific Transylvanian dialect is incontestable proof of their Romanian origin. Except for a few lexical elements of Szeckler origin, due to their living alongside the Szecklers for a long period of time, their Romanian dialect contains no sound in its phonetical system that could be considered to be a Szeckler origin. On the contrary, their Hungarian dialect, spoken by a small minority, for instance in Săbăoani (in the county of Neamţ), preserved numerous phonemes of Romanian origin, due to which the phonetical system of this dialect cannot be considered Hungarian.

With regard to the emigrations during the eighteenth century, we mention here the declaration made by the bishop of Bacău, Stanislau Jezierski, in 1763, saying that the number of Catholics in Moldavia was constantly increasing through those coming from Transylvania.[2] And Petru Zöld, as we have already seen, found three years later that the number of Catholics in Moldavia, called by him Changos, who, however, had only recently arrived from Transylvania, were bilingual, speaking Romanian and not very good Hungarian, and were wearing Romanian costumes.

It goes without saying that, after these people had established themselves in Moldavia, given the new social, political, and religious conditions, the process of Szecklerization weakened and later ceased. Being used less and less, as it no longer answered any necessities, the Hungarian Chango dialect quickly disappeared in most of the villages. Despite the efforts made by the few Hungarian missionaries in Moldavia, the inevitable could not be avoided. The Hungarian dialect disappeared and together with it the corrupted pronunciation of its speakers. Linguistically speaking, the so-called Changos disappeared; Romanians remained, speaking their traditional Romanian language.

---

[2]G. Călinescu, *Alte notizie*, p. 476.

In 1844, the Hungarian pilgrim Jernei János noted that the Hungarian language had disappeared or was on the point of disappearing in most of the villages. Here and there, some of the old people still remember some Hungarian words.[3] Some Hungarian authors saw its disappearance as a serious national loss. One brochure in which the Moldavian Romanians are accused of forcibly denationalizing "the poor Magyar Changos," characterizes Moldavia as a "great cemetery for the Hungarians."[4] These affirmations, however, are xenophobic, as the Changos renounced the Hungarian dialect, which they only recently acquired, through a natural and voluntary process, preferring to speak their native Romanian dialect.

It is true that in recent times many of them have acquired the Moldavian dialect as well, with the result that they now speak two distinct dialects. With strangers they speak in the Moldavian dialect, and at home, with their families, they speak in their specific Transylvanian dialect. By settling in Moldavia, the Changos did not lose their language or their nationality, but, on the contrary, they saved their Romanian language and nationality threatened by Szecklerization in Transylvania. They saved their ethnic identity, which their conationals who remained in Transylvania lost, most of them being assimilated by the Szecklers.

As for the bilingual Changos, in some villages, especially in the county of Bacău, the inhabitants, who had undergone a more profound

---

[3] Jernei János, *Keleti utázasa* (A trip to the East), I, Pesten, 1851, p. 25.

[4] Baumgartner Sándor, *Moldva a magyarság nagy temetöje*, Budapest, 1940, p. 32 (Editor's Note: Regarding the sinister metaphor which appears in the title of the leaflet, also used in the past by Aladár Ballaghi, we should mention the fact that in his article "A moldvai magyarok," published in the magazine *Kárpátmedence* (I, 1941, Sept.), in which he refers to the yeomen's class as a Magyar institution, the same author, signing only with the initials of his name, unthinkingly writes that "it is not half a million Szecklers of Romanian origin who have been made Magyars" but rather "almost a million Magyars in Moldavia who have been made Romanians" (p. 301).

process of Szecklerization before coming to Moldavia, speak Hungarian Chango dialect at home, and when speaking to others they speak Romanian. These Changos can be found in villages like Lespezi, Valea Seacă, Valea Mare, Fărăoani, Cleja, Galbeni, Gioseni, Găidar, Nicolae Bălcescu, Luizi-Călugăra, Pustiana, Ploscuţeni (in the southern group), Săbăoani and Pildeşti (in the northern group).[5] This population of Hungarian language is not of Hungarian ethnicity, as many have claimed. It is a population of Romanian origin that underwent a more profound process of Szecklerization from a linguistic point of view. All the traditional ethnographic elements of this population remained Romanian their costume, traditions, way of life, the type of houses they live in, the hearth, the wedding ceremony, the cast-iron kettle for hominy, the stove shelf, the round table with three legs, the weaving loom, the interior of their homes, the hope chest, etc. for the ethnographer and even for the uninitiated person, it is sufficient to look at the images in the two volumes by Péter Pál Domokos and László Mikecs to convince themselves that this population is incontestably Romanian, and that the process of Szecklerization did not change anything from the viewpoint of their material life and artistic creations.[6] Although these inhabitants, especially the old women speak the Hungarian Chango dialect at home, they preserve the tradition that they are different from real Hungarians.

In the social and political circumstances in Transylvania in the past, they were assimilated from a linguistic point of view. The

---

[5]At Săbăoani, except Licuşeni, the northern part of the village, where only Romanian is spoken; at Pildeşti, the Hungarian language is spoken only by old people.

[6]See also the recent book on the folk art of the Changos in Moldavia, published Kós Károly, Szentimrei Judit, and Dr. Nagy Jenö which, through its subject and illustrations, vividly proves their Romanian origin.

Szecklers also gave to and received from them folklore,[7] but psychologically and spiritually, as far as their way of life, traditions, and artistic creations are concerned, they never ceased being Romanians. When faced with the situation of choosing between two alternatives and free of any constraint, they opt, without hesitation, for their Romanian traditions, whose roots go very deep in their historical past.[8]

In those approximately 150 villages, out of which around 70 compact ones representing about 70% of the total of the Catholic population in Moldavia, the inhabitants forgot the Hungarian language long ago and speak only Romanian, and, what is essential and significant when discussing the question of their origins, they speak Romanian in their specific Transylvanian dialect. When they arrived from Transylvania, many of them settled down in the villages mentioned by Bandinus (Săbăoani, Talpa, Buruieneşti, Sagna, Rotunda, Butea, Oţeleni, etc.). Later on, leaving these larger villages, they founded new villages further east, in the regions of Cârligătura and Iaşi.

After emigrating to Moldavia, these peaceful and hard-working people led their lives unhindered by anyone, speaking Romanian in their traditional dialect and living according to their century-old customs. The fact that some people in Moldavia considered them foreigners or that others from abroad claimed them as part of the Hungarian nation were problems that did not interest them. What was essential for their peace was that no one forced them to speak a foreign language any longer, no one prevented them from living according to

---

[7]See Farago Iosef, "Variantele maghiare ale Mioriţei" ("The Magyar Versions of *Mioriţa*"), in *Limbă şi Literatură*, V, 1961, pp. 357-369.

[8]About their attitude toward the schools with Hungarian as teaching language, founded after 1948, see supra, p. 14.

their traditions, and no one ridiculed them for wearing Romanian clothes. Their Catholicism, which was now Romanian, had not changed their nature, or their customs, or their way of life.[9] Settled

---

[9](Editor's Note) If, owing to historical circumstances, Catholicism in the region peopled by Szecklers took on a Magyar aspect, Catholicism in Moldavia was Romanian in its structure, deeply rooted in the country's history, supported and even embraced by the ruling class, at least until the Phanariot period. In Moldavia, the proto-Romanian Latin Christianity, which had been interrupted by the Slavonic influence, adapted itself to the new circumstances (until the linguistic reform in the Church, whoever saw Moldavian Catholics dressed in white and singing in a choir in Latin had the feeling that he was living in the primary epoch of Christianity) under the form of Catholicism, present here ab antiquo. Catholicism "adjusted itself to the Romanian circumstances, identified itself with the interests of this country, became native, and took on a national aspect, so to say" (Alex. Lapedatu, *Noul regim al cultelor din România*, Bucureşti, 1928, p. 11), the Roman-Catholic Church being considered a national church (see I. Dumitriu-Snagov, op. cit., pp. 493-494, 585). Crossing the Carpathians, the Catholic Romanians from the Magyarized region strengthened their national being and the Romanian language, thus developing the national character of Catholicism in Moldavia.

Before the Phanariot period, there had been no conflicts between Orthodoxy and Catholicism, but they existed side by side in "such a great harmony… that even the clergy of the two big religions had almost forgotten the discord which had torn apart Christ's church" (M. Kogălniceanu, the speech made in the Ad-hoc Council on 25 Oct, 1857; see *Opere*, III/I, p. 41). In fact, officially, the Orthodox Church in Moldavia never retracted the Union pact which had been signed by the Metropolitan Bishop Damian, in Florence, in 1439. Furthermore, for papal Rome, the Moldavian voievods retained the halo surrounding the figure of Stephen the Great, whom Pope Sixtus IV called "an athlete of faith," due to his bravery in the struggles against the Turks. For more details about the relations between Moldavia and Rome see: C. Auner, *Moldova la soborul din Florenţa*, ed. II, Bucureşti, 1915 (excerpt from *Revista catolică*); Ioan Ferenţ, "Petru Şchiopul şi catolicismul in Moldova," in *Calendarul catolic*, XII, 1914, pp. 59-63; idem, "Ieremia Movilă (1595-1606) şi catolicismul," ibidem, XIII, 1915, pp. 37-49; Chiril Karalevski, "Relaţiunile dintre domnii români şi Sfântul Scaun în a doua jumătate a veacului al XVI-lea după documente inedite din Arhivele Vaticanului," in *Revista catolică*, II, 1913, nr. 2-4, III, 1914, p. 2; Ioan Al. Roth S.I., "Silinţele de unire în Moldova cătră sfârşitul veacului al XVI-lea," in *Unirea* (Blaj), X, 1900, nr. 7-13; Mons. Aloise L. Tăutu, "Spirit 'ecumenie' între papalitate şi români pe vremea lui Ştefan cel Mare," in *Buna vestire* (Roma), IV, 1965, nr. 1, pp. 4-11, and

down and irrevocably integrated into the spiritual and social climate of Moldavia,[10] living in harmony with the Moldavians, among whom some were of the same religion, speaking the same language that they did, they became more and more conscious of what they were and had never ceased to be, of the fact that they were Romanians, just as the Moldavians, that they spoke the *same language.*

The Hungarian author Rózsa Ignácz, who traveled through Moldavia, noted with melancholy the complete absence of the Hungarian consciousness and the vigorous Romanian patriotism of the inhabitants of Luizi-Călugăra (in the county of Bacău). She noted these facts and deplored them, but the traditional essence of their Romanian spirit escaped her understanding. Like many Hungarian nationalists, Rózsa Ignácz maintained the illusion of their pure Magyar origin. The author ignored the Szecklerization that took place in Transylvania, and the Romanian origin of the Changos and deplored their fate, as usual, in plaintive tones.[11]

Unfortunately, some Romanian scholars did not perceive the historical drama of this population, or the real historical-linguistic essence of the Chango phenomenon. Even today, some Romanian scholars look with skepticism upon the "naive" presumption of some

---

XIV, 1975, nr. 1, pp. 335-34; M. Theordorian-Carada, *Papa*, Bucureşti, 1906, pp. 118-13; ed. II, Iaşi, 1938, pp. 129-157.

[10]Two attestations from the beginning of the twentieth century: "There are no Catholics here. But wherever they are, we get along well with them. They live as we do. But most of them are merchants and farmers" (I.A. Candrea, Ov. Densusianu, Th.D. Sperantia, *Graiul nostrum*, I, Bucureşti, 1906, p. 471). "They are Catholics but they are not bad people" (ibidem, p. 824).

[11]Rózsa Ignácz, *Keleti magyarik nyomaban* (In the Footsteps of the Hungarian in the East), Budapest, 1941, pp. 72-73.

Changos who consider themselves to be Romanians.[12] Nor did the authorities in the not so distant past have a clear vision of the situation of these inhabitants. This explains the initiative of the authorities to organize Hungarian schools for them in the county of Bacău.[13] No matter how great the zeal of the Szeckler teachers, who came from Transylvania, the schools closed because of a lack of students. *Do you want to turn us into Hungarians?* The people asked in bewilderment to those who went from house to house to convince them to participate in the experiment. They knew they were Romanians and wanted Romanian schools.

Unfortunately, researchers in Romanian institutes (historians, linguists, sociologists, and folklorists) have usually avoided the Catholic villages of Moldavia.[14] Linguists especially neglected to

---

[12]See Pr. Serafin M. Bejan, "Catolicii din Moldova," in *Almanahul... "Viaţa"*, 1924, p. 26; Iosif Ghiuzan, "Român catolic," in *Santinela catolică*, VI, 1928, nr. 10, oct., pp. 1-2.

[13](Editor's Note) What happened in Moldavia between 1948 and 1950 is closely related to previous attempts initiated abroad and mentioned by Bonaventura M. Morariu and Pietro Tocanel, Moldavian Franciscan priests who had settled in Italy, in Memoriale sui tentativi dell' Ungheria di mandare sacerdoti in Moldavia, which was submitted to Pope Pius XII on 1 September 1946, in the name of the monks from Romania. The authors present the history of all the attempts at Magyarizing the Catholics in Moldavia and ask the pope to pay no heed to the Hungarian chauvinists as these believers are Romanian people by right and origin, and they all speak Romanian. The statement that the present clergy in Moldavia, being Romanian, has no idea of their language and feelings, and thus is incapable of satisfying their spiritual needs, is contrary to the entire history and present situation, the secular and regular priests being raised from among the people. See the text of the memo at Petru Tocănel, "Franciscanii minori conventuali şi limba română," in *Buna vestire*, Roma XI, 1972, nr. 3, iul.-sept., pp. 39-43; for more details about the attempts at Magyarization during the eighteenth and nineteenth centuries see idem, *Storia della Chiesa Cattolica in Romania*, III, pp. 18-93, 331-347.

[14](Editor's Note) Mărtinaş is right, but only with respect to the villages in which Romanian was spoken, that is, the majority, as the villages with bilingual population have been the object of many studies and much research during the past forty years,

study their Romanian dialect, which is full of Transylvanian elements, something detrimental to scholarship.[15]

The lack of interest by Romanian scholars for the Chango phenomenon harmed the Changos most, as the Romanians continued to consider them as foreigners, despite the fact that they knew themselves to be Romanians. Rulers in the past were interested in them only from an economic perspective (for taxes and statute labor). Despite the indifference of the state, they found in their tradition the Romanian essence that G. Popa-Lisseanu was talking about,[16] they found the power to rid themselves of Hungarian influences and to remain Romanians. When the schools of Spiru Haret appeared in their villages, at the beginning of the twentieth century, there was no one to be "assimilated" by these schools, because they were Romanians and spoke Romanian when they were still in Transylvania. Today the consciousness of their Romanian belonging is strong and active, as they have proven in many difficult circumstances.[17] As in the past,

---

from a Magyar perspective, of course, at the "Babeş-Bolyai" University, the Institute of Linguistics, and the Ethnographic Museum of Transylvania, all in Cluj. Numerous articles and studies about the few bilingual Changos have been published in both Romanian and Magyar, especially in the fields of linguistics, ethnography, and folklore; on the other hand, no one has dealt with the Changos who speak Romanian, from any perspective.

[15]One example: specialists have established that /l'/ (palatal) was transformed into /i/, in Dacian-Romanian, already in the sixteenth century. However, in certain villages of the northern group one still hears pronunciations like: l'eu, l'ei, l'e (<Lat.); for example: l'e sama, l'e mâna, for ia seama, ia mâna (pay attention, move your hand).

[16]See infra, p. 57.

[17](Editor's Note) Here is an account of a lesser known situation which occurred during the military dictatorship. In 1942-1943, the leading authorities sought to effect a change of population between Romanians and Hungarians. The latter also included the so-called Changos, whose parents, sons, and brothers, were on the front at that time (a similar proposal regarding the exchange of Romanians living in Hungary for Changos living in Moldavia was made by the newspaper *Nemzeti ujsáj* on 7 February 1937). Learning of what was foreseen, Bishop Mihai Robu appealed to the French

they constantly manifest their disapproval toward those who consider them to be of foreign origin.

The study of language and history prove, with undeniable linguistic data and facts, that their tradition regarding the Romanian ethnicity has a strong linguistic and historical foundation.[18] Linguistic research has succeeded in removing the opaque veil that covered, until recently, the so-called enigma of the Changos. Research in this field has brought to light the Transylvanian historical-linguistic antecedents, forgotten or ignored by historians, and have situated this controversial phenomenon in its original social and historical context, in the history of the Romanians in southeast-Transylvania. In the difficult historical

---

government, through the Apostolic Nuncio Andrea Cassulo, sending the following message: "If we have to leave the country, then another Latin country should receive us, 100,000 believers, 30,000 of whom are good workers and 10,000 are good fighters" (this fact was recounted to Dumitru Mărtinaş by the bishop himself, in 1943; see *Caietul* XV, pp. 71-73). The matter was soon dropped. Moreover, Mihai Antonescu, vice-president of the Council of Ministers, ordered that the local governments release certificates attesting to the Romanian nationality of the Changos (before this period, these certificates were released with no difficulty). The prefecture of the country of Roman transmitted this order on 23 August 1943, referring to it as order no. 13038, and ending it with these words: "This measure is necessary for putting an end to the grievances among the Catholic population in Moldavia which have to be taken into account as they are justified by political and historical realities" (excerpt from the collection P. Iosif Simon of Huşi).

[18](Editor's Note) Ioan Mărtinaş wrote in 1944: "We hope that a time will come when science, based not only on blood testing, but on other data as well, will bear out the Romanian character of the Moldavians Catholics. Thus, the objective history of these worthy citizens, the sacrifices made in national wars, their specifically Romanian costume, their names, customs, and especially their Romanian dialect, containing sounds which remind us of the old vulgar Latin, -- all these demonstrate the authentic Romanian character of the Catholic population in Moldavia. The Hungarian dialect itself, which is still heard in some villages, especially in the county of Bacău, is an amazing proof of their Romanian origin. Indeed, a careful examination – both philological and phonetical – proves that this people spoke Romanian first and only later learned Hungarian" ("Sunt ciangăii români?," in *Lumina creştinului*, XXX, 1944, ian., p. 29).

conditions of the past, many Changos were forced to flee to Moldavia in search of a better life.

Just as the Romanian people, surrounded by more powerful nations, living for centuries separated into different states and under different foreign rulers, managed to preserve throughout history their spiritual unity and ethnic consciousness thanks mainly to their language, in the same way this population, due to their language brought from Transylvania, managed to preserve their ethnic-linguistic individuality and sentiments of solidarity with the language and destiny of the Romanian nation to which they belong.

Chapter 10

A New Process of Magyarization (The Nineteenth Century)

The immediate result of the emigration of the Changos to Moldavia was that in the new social and political conditions the consequences of the process of Szecklerization they underwent in Transylvania gradually faded, eventually disappearing completely almost everywhere, especially in the villages of the northern group.

This fact was brought to the knowledge of the bishop of Transylvania who, as we have already seen, appealed in 1787 to Pope Pius VI for the replacement of the Italian missionaries with Hungarian ones. Knowing that in the Catholic churches in Moldavia the Romanian language was necessary, the pope did not approve the bishop's request, and the Italian missionaries remained to do their duty. On the other hand, for the minority speaking the Hungarian language, he ordered that the primate of Hungary, send to Franciscan priests. But the bishop and the Magyar clergymen were not pleased with the pope's decision. They remained firm in their conviction that all Catholics in Moldavia had to be pastored in the Magyar language. They waited for a more favorable moment to propose again this idea.

An unexpected circumstance allowed the Hungarian ecclesiastical leadership to resume more energetically their offensive against the

Romanian language spoken by the Catholic believers. During the time of Bishop

Ioan Filip Paroni, the Fide Propaganda Congregation was unable to send to Moldavia the personnel necessary to staff the mission.[1] In this situation, the bishop thought that he should ask for the help of the province of the Conventual Franciscans in Transylvania. In 1825, an agreement was concluded between Bishop Paroni and the respective provincial organization, through which the province obliged itself to place a number of six priests at the disposal of the mission, in exchange for a hundred *scuzi* annually. These Hungarian priests would work in Moldavia for the next forty years.

The Hungarian missionaries were convinced that all Catholic believers in Moldavia were and had to remain Hungarians forever, having thus the duty to know and to speak Hungarian. But when they came to Moldavia they were shocked to find that most of the believers did not know any Hungarian, that they talked among themselves only in Romanian, and that they were resistant to the Hungarian language. When, occasionally, some old people tried to speak Hungarian, they pronounced the words so badly that they were not even understood by the missionaries. Seeing this, the missionaries began to alert the ecclesiastical authorities in Hungary, saying that in Moldavia the Hungarian language was disappearing, and with it the Catholic religion.

All the Hungarian missionaries, scholars, and journalists of those times saw this natural process of forgetting the Hungarian language as a result of a policy of denationalization. They accused the Moldavians of forcibly Romanianizing the "poor Magyar Changos" and attacked

---

[1](Editor's Note) This fact was also determined by the tense relations between Bishop Paroni and the superiors of the Minor Conventual Franciscan order in Rome, and the suggestion for this solution was given by Lippas, the new Austrian consular agent in Iaşi (see Iosif Gabor, *Ierarhia catolică a Moldovei*, III, p. 26).

the Italian missionaries, claiming that, instead of seeing to the salvation of souls, they concerned themselves with Romanianizing their parishioners. Influenced by their own Romantic nationalism, they could not see in Moldavia anything but denationalization and assimilation by force.

What was really happening? The state, which, like everyone else, considered the Changos to be a Hungarian population, was indifferent to these "foreigners" and did not take much interest in their fate. But something more important was happening. The Changos, who were said to have been assimilated completely by the Moldavians, in reality did not speak Romanian in the Moldavian dialect, they had not acquired the dialect of the Moldavians, but were speaking in their specific Transylvanian dialect inherited from their Romanian ancestors. Even today, in their families, they speak their old Romanian dialect. Therefore, they were not Romanianized by force by "intolerant" Romanian governments, nor were they assimilated by the Moldavians. If the Changos from a century ago spoke Romanian in the Transylvanian dialect, as do the Changos today, this was due to the fact that they were of Romanian origin. This fact becomes even more obvious when we consider that many of them, for example those in Valea Seacă (in the county of Bacău) or in Hălăuceşti (today in the county of Iaşi), were Greek-Catholic Romanians, who, emigrating to Moldavia, in the absence of their Church, adopted the Roman rite. This did not prevent some authors from identifying the village of Valea Seacă as one of the largest Hungarian villages in the county of Bacău.[2]

---

[2]Iosif Petru M. Pal, op. cit., p. 52 (Editor's Note: In a note to the Propaganda, in 1745, it was mentioned: Il rito de' Cristiani în q(ues) ta Provincia una buona parte e Ap(ostoli)co Romano, altri sono Greci Cattolici uniti, altri sono Armeni Cattolici del Rito Greco (G. Călinescu, *Alcuni misionari*, p. 185).

When Bishop Paroni invited the Hungarian missionaries to Moldavia, he did not imagine the problems that would result because of them. As soon as they arrived there they became propagandists for the Hungarian language among resistant parishioners. It was a tragic error, a serious misunderstanding of the historical and linguistic situation, which damaged the spiritual work of the mission.

In the villages they were assigned to, these missionaries set out to work with determination. They began with the parochial registers: *liber baptizatorum, liber copulatorum, liber defunctorum.*[3] During a time when the authority of the priest in the parish was not disputed by anyone, when control by the civil authorities was non-existent, he involved himself in the affairs of the community to whatever extent he desired. Associating himself with the psalm reader,[4] usually a Szeckler

---

[3](Editor's Note) Here are some Catholic parished in Moldavia where rolls since the seventeenth century have been preserved: Luizi-Călugăra (since 1773), Adjudeni (since 1775), Hălăuceşti (since 1780), Faraoani (since 1780, according to Îndrumător, 1789, according to Schematismus), Cleja (since 1793), Săbăoani (since 1797). (See P. Joseph P.M. Pal, *Schematismus fratrum minorum, passim, and Îndrumător în Arhivele Statului. Judeţul Bacău*, Bucureşti, 1979, p. 289). Page 283 reads: "The rolls made by the Catholic parishes provide many opportunities for arguing in favor of the Romanian ethnic origin of the Catholic population living in Moldavia." Thus, the statements according to which the oldest rolls found in Moldavia and Wallachia so far belong to the Orthodox denomination (since 1829) and that the other denominations have not preserved any old rolls are both wrong (see Liviu Moldovan, "Înregistrarea de către biserici a botezurilor, cununaţilor şi înmormîntaţilor în ţările române în secolele XVIII-XIX," in *Populaţie şi societate*, III, Cluj-Napoca, 1980, p. 138; however, in the same volume, p. 144, Ecaterina Negruţ, *Les dossiers paroisseaux de Moldavie et leurs importance comme source démographique*, provides exact information in this respect.

[4](Editor's Note) Because of the lack of priests in the past, the church singers enjoyed a great deal of authority in the Catholic communities. Bandinus relates that a church singer "is regarded as superior to both the bishop and the sacred host of cardinals" (V.A. Urechia, *Codex Bandinus*, p. 153). For more details about the tasks of a church singer, see Iosif Malinovski, *Manualul dascălului catolic*, Iaşi, 1908; about the schools for church singers in Moldavia see Iosif Petru M. Pál, *op. cit.*, pp. 209-213.

brought from Transylvania, complying with the well-known official practice, the missionary would bring with him the revision, that is the "purification" and Magyarization of the church records. The names of the parishioners were translated into Hungarian, according to the wishes of the priest and his collaborator, the Szeckler psalm reader. Thus, family names like: *Lupu, Negrea, Rotaru, Feraru* became *Farkas, Fekete, Kerekes, Kovács,* and so on. Other times, the family name was eliminated and replaced with the first name translated into Hungarian: *Gavril Avădanei* was changed into *Gábor, Anton Prisăcaru* into *Antal, Mihai Rusu* into *Mihály, Pavel Dumitraş* into *Pál.*[5]

Little by little, due to the Magyarizing zeal of the missionaries, the original names of the parishioners had become mixed with Hungarian names which they often did not even understand. No one understood why *Floarea* had become *Virág,* why *Ursaru* had become *Medvés,* why *Bujor* was now *Bozsó.* The name of the village was also changed in the registers, so *Barticeşti* all of a sudden became *Barikok.*[6]

---

[5]See *ibidem,* p. 53.

[6](Leopold Nestmann), *Cronica parohiei Barticeşti,* i, p. 160 (a manuscript preserved in the Catholic parish of Barticeşti, in the county of Neamţ. (Editor's Note: Here is a convincing excerpt from a German author: "Under him (under priest Iosif Kónia, who came from Transylvania after the convention of Bishop Paroni), the rolls in Hălăuceşti change so fast that you have the impression that you are suddenly in another country... in Hungary as it were. He changed even the name of our village, listing it as 'Bartikok'... Several names cannot be even identified any more. For instance, how can one (who is not familiar with the previous registrations) know that Buszó is the name, so widely-spread nowadays and so Romanian, for Bujor?" (pp. 160-161). Recall also the metamorphosis Dumitraş-Pál. "In 1871 the roll of the parish in Hălăceşti refers to my grandfather in the following way: Petrus Pauli Dumitraş is registered as Anton Petru Pál. And since that year all members of Petru Dumitraş's family have been known as Pál! What has been left of our real name? And who was so smart as to substitute the Hungarian Pál for Dumitraş? (Iosif Petru M. Pál, op. cit., p. 53). "And now we raise the following question to those who, no matter if they are Romanians or Hungarians, accept the theory of the Hungarian origin of the Changos: what is the

Another bold endeavor of Magyarization was the attempt to replace the Romanian language in the church, which had a centuries-old tradition in Moldavia, with the Hungarian language.[7] The reading

---

reason for this hasty and systematic Magyarization of Romanian names borne by Catholic Changos by the Hungarian priests? Is this the sign of their Magyar origin? Or is this proof of their Romanian origin, a proof which had to be wiped away as soon as possible?" (D. Mărtinaş, *Caietul Alfa,* p. 145).

[7](Editor's Note) With regard to the conflict over the language used in the religious service and the prevalence of Romanian in the Catholic villages in Moldavia, a visitor, General Iosif Tomassi (1858), observed: "Now it is all a matter of the language in which the sermon will be officiated, for this is the main problem which caused and still causes the conflict of opinions among missionaries, a conflict which divided them and still does into two opposing groups: the Hungarians and the Italians. The first claim that their language has to take precedence, and moreover, to become the only language to be used in these missionary activities and – starting from this assumption – they not only explain the Gospel and preach in Hungarian, but they also prevent the believers from speaking Moldavian, saying that it is a schismatic language. The others – on the contrary – care more for the Moldavian language; this is the language that they learn, that they use for preaching and in administering their parishes.

This is why a great rivalry grew up among them, the most vehement instigator being the priest Petras, who – although he speaks Moldavian very well – never says a word in this language. In the past, this rivalry caused many disputes. Such things no longer take place today, the reason being the presence of Italian missionaries, who do not put up any blatant resistance to their opponents. However, rivalry exists and – for the sake of the faithful – it should stop, so that they can share the spiritual food in the most known and common language.

If someone asked my opinion, I could express it without any doubt, because I have thoroughly examined this problem, and therefore, I am happy to state, without being prejudiced against any national group, that the language which should come first in this mission is the Moldavian one, and that Hungarian should not be excluded either as it can also be useful. It's true that I know neither of these languages, and I could not ask any of the believers. However, I agree with those missionaries who steer clear from the conflict between the two groups. I've also asked some Hungarians because, after all, not all of them are fanatic. I've also talked to the church singers, who all speak Latin, and they have told me that many people speak Hungarian, but that Moldavian is spoken by all of them, including the Hungarians. Moreover, although I – as I've already told you – do not speak these languages, after four months of uninterrupted traveling through Moldavia, I have come to know almost all the

of the Gospel and the sermon were done in Hungarian, different hymns and litanies were sung in Hungarian, and the psalm reader was teaching the catechism in Hungarian as well.

The trouble was, however, that the presumed "Hungarians" did not know Hungarian. They complained to the priest that they did not understand anything, but he had a different opinion. He was preaching in Hungarian so that those who did not know this language might learn it, and those who knew it might not forget it. Because the people were complaining, the priest formed a few partisans from among those who understood him, who would try to convince the people that they had to pray in Hungarian, so that God would listen and receive their prayers better. In time, two rival factions formed in the villages: one favoring the Romanian language and the other favoring the Hungarian language. As a result, the arguments were endless, becoming more and more heated, sometimes breaking out even in church.[8]

---

believers living there. And, although I did not understand what they said, I could tell, by sounds and accents, what language they used, and thus I became convinced that Moldavian is the language spoken by all the believers living in that province, and I could not say the same thing about Hungarian" (see Iosif Gabor, *Ierarhia catolică a Moldovei*, III, p. 87, manuscript; I. Dumitru-Snagov, op. cit., pp. 376-377).

The dominance of the Romanian language in the Catholic villages in Moldavia is also proven by the mention of *usus linguae* in "Prospectus missions romano-catholicae in Moldavia existentis," in *Kalendarium franciscano-romano-julianum...* Iaşi, 1850, pp. 41-47.

[8](Editor's Note) Situations like this were repeated for a short time after 1948, as well. here is an account given by an eye-witness, the schoolteacher Mihai Gherguţă, who was a regional school inspector in the county of Bacău at the time: "The agitators, who came from among Szecklers, urged some Catholic citizens to demand that the religious service be officiated in Magyar. Most of the Catholic believers insisted that the religious service should be officiated as before. In some localities, the inhabitants were divided into two opposing groups which indulged in beatings and scuffles. A disturbance was raised in the village of Lespezi (in the county of Bacău), where order was threatened. The county authorities were informed by some peaceful inhabitants and they sent a dispute committee there... The discussions with people from both

The petitions and complaints were arriving in ever larger numbers of the apostolic representative in Iaşi. Sometimes they were addressed to the regional authorities, and sometimes they went all the way to Rome. But the Hungarian missionaries did not just sit and wait: they kept alerting the government and the ecclesiastical authorities.

The superiors in Iaşi tried hard to settle the conflicts, urging the people to be peaceful and the missionaries to be moderate. The chancelleries of the Fide Propaganda Congregation and of the nunciature in Vienna were informed about the problems that had arisen in the mission in Moldavia.

If before, in Transylvania, the possibility of insubordination before the priest had not existed, in Moldavia the situation was completely different. There the voices of the people were freer and more determined. They understood, after a while, that the missionary priests were plotting against them. First they changed their names without asking them, and now they wanted to change their language as well. Their murmurs became protests, determining the regional authorities to use public force to maintain peace and order in church.

The bishops regretted very much the imprudence that was made when the Hungarian missionaries were sent to Moldavia. It was not easy, however, to discipline these missionaries, to administer them a canonical sanction, or to send them away, because they would immediately send petitions to Vienna. Since 1814 Austria had been the protector of the Catholic mission in Moldavia and therefore one could not easily ignore the authority of the Austrian consul in Iaşi. After a time, he also realized that the zeal of the Hungarian missionaries had

---

sides – who were brought face to face – took hours. Conflicts were stirred in many villages, where agitators talked some people into introducing the Magyar language in church" (from the letter quoted).

gone too far, agitating uselessly a peaceful population and thus becoming suspicious and detestable in the eyes of the State authorities.

In connection with this problem there was an exchange of letters between Bishop Paul Sardi in Iaşi and Cardinal Iosif Kopácsy, the primate of Hungary, which can be found in Nicolae Iorga's *Studii şi documente*, I-II.[9]

Sardi complains about the behavior of some missionaries, who, "driven by the blind national fanaticism" (*caeco nationalitatis fanatismo abrepti*), make common cause with some political agitators who came here from Hungary and provoke revolts and discords among the population. Only the intervention of the diplomatic agent Eisenoach prevented the decree of expulsion of the Hungarian missionaries from being published and carried out.[10]

Combining a political mission with their religious one, and seeing the Italian missionaries as an impediment to their Magyarization plans, the Hungarian missionaries constantly tried to eliminate the Italians and transform the Catholic mission in Moldavia into a Hungarian one. Hoping for the assistance of the government in Vienna and setting forth mainly spiritual reasons, they thought that they would be able to convince the Roman Curia to approve the removal of the Italian missionaries. But the Fide Propaganda Congregation, understanding very well this delicate problem, refused to accept their proposal.

Convinced that an honest and harmonious collaboration with the Franciscan Hungarian province and with its missionaries could not be realized by any means, on 17 July 1859, the general representative, Iosif Tomassi, informed his superiors of the Franciscan order in Rome

---

[9]See pp. 221-224. On 30 November 1845, Sardi sent to Rome the original of the last letter of the Hungarian Cardinal, characterizing it as follows: *Un' amalgama di fanatismo e di contradizioni siffate... un' affare do mala fede* (ibidem, p. 224).

[10]See the letter to Kopacsy dated 24 October 1845 (ibidem, p. 222).

that in the future the sum of a hundred *scuzi* would not be sent any longer to the Hungarian Franciscan provincial, but to the "San Antonio" college in Rome, for two Italian missionaries, because the convention of Bishop Paroni had become not only onerous (*onerosa*), but even undignified (*indecorosa*). "And this is how he eradicated right from the root the seed of discord and re-established the peace of the mission," concluded a Romanian Franciscan historian born in Moldavia.[11]

If the cancellation of the convention and the gradual withdrawal of the Hungarian missionaries from Moldavia re-established the peace of the mission, the negative effects of their activities are still felt today. When, during the rule of Alexandru Ioan Cuza, the Romanian state organized the registers of births, marriages, and deaths, and established that they should be kept in the city and village halls, the local officials began copying the data from the church registers, as they had been "purified" by the Hungarian missionaries.[12] The old historical names of the Changos had been Magyarized first in

---

[11]Atque sic denique semen dissensus penitus extirpavit, pacemque in missione stabilivit (Bonaventura Morariu, *Series chrologica episcoporum ac praefectorum apostolicorum Missionis, fratrum minorum conventualium in Moldavia (Romania) durante saeculo XIX*, Roma, 1942, pp. 11-12). (Editor's Note: See also the appendix to the information provided by Iosif Toma of feud" had been removed, but the slow process of Magyarization continued. Pointing to the decree of Pope Clement XIV, on 21 March 1774, which referred to the missionaries' obligation to learn the language of the people, Almanacul cultelor in 1868 wrote that its strict enforcement "might soon put an end to the incessant process of Magyarization – involving so many villages – through Hungarian priests who speak only Magyar" (*Acte şi notiţii relative la cultul catolic*, pp. 118-119).

[12]Two curiosities concerning names from Butea (in the county of Iaşi) are worth mentioning. When names were transcribed from the church rolls, the notary also found abbreviated names: *Giurgi M-ai Antal, Anton M-ai Mihai (M-ai* being the shortened form for *Mihai*), which he lead and wrote as if they were tied: *Maiantal* and *Măimihai*, which became family names. On this occasion, many Hungarian family names became official, such as: *Pál, Antál, Gábor, Cherecheş*, etc. (D. Mărtinaş, *Caietul XI*, p. 310).

Transylvania, then, for the second time, in Moldavia, without the knowledge and consent of those concerned. These names, which have become official, obligatory today, are mixed with many names of Hungarian origin, which correspond neither to the language, nor the traditions, nor the preferences of the population. Often these people expressed their discontent regarding this situation, wanting to change it, but did not succeed, either because of their lack of the necessary means or because of procedural difficulties.[13]

---

[13](Editor's Note) A lesser known aspect should be mentioned here: "The Hungarian names given to the Moldavian families are used only in writing, for people pronounce them as in Romanian; for instance, *Medveş* is known to people only by the name of *Ursu*" (Iosif Gabor, *Tămăşeni, file din trecut*, p. 99; manuscript preserved at the Catholic parish in Tămăşeni, in the county of Neamţ).

The nicknames are all Romanian: Aciobănoaie, Agăinoaie, Ambiţie, Aturcului, Badea Fugă, Balanu, Bodolan, Boghean, Borcan, Bot-de-iepure, Budac (fem. Budacica), Buftea, Buium, Burcă, Chiper, Cişleag, Chitan, Cizmariu (fem. Cizmăroaia), Cocostârc, Conea (fem. Coneasa and Conoaia), Cozonac (fem. Cozonăciţa), Craiu (fem. Crăiasa), Crâstea, Cucoş, Cucu, Dâgdă, Drug, Frumuşica (fem), Furatu, Găină, Geandră, Giurgoiaie, Gândăcel (fem. Gândăcica), Gât-Strâmb, Glonţu, Guleanu, Hostolomei, Înfietu (fem. Înfietoaia), Mama-Ceea, Pitrica, Pucea, Scrob, Stuchici, Surdan, Turtă, etc. (examples taken from Sagna, in the county of Neamţ).

Chapter 11

Historical and Ethnographic Considerations

Albis induti vestibus

–The register of the Monastery of Şumuleu, 1783

To support the thesis of the Romanian origin of the Changos we have often appealed to ethnographic arguments as well, which could constitute the object of a special study.[1] But since the ethnographic

---

[1]See Iosif Petru, *op. cit.,* pp. 55-65. (Editor's Note: According to the traveler named László, interesting ethnographic data can be found in the idyllic description made by Attila de Gerando, "Les Tschangos," in *Revue de géographie,* Paris, XII, 1878, volume III, July-Dec., pp. 282-288. It is useful, in this context, to present a study published by Kós Károly, an ethnographer from Cluj, who began his research in Moldavia in 1949. The article is entitled "Csángó néprajzi vázlat" ("Etnographical Sketch of the Changos"), and appeared in the volume *Tajak, falvak, hagyomaniok* (*Regions, Villages, Customs*), Bucureşti, 1976, pp. 103-217. It includes extensive information on the material culture of the Catholic population in a few Moldavian villages. As is natural, one encounters Romanian aspects every step of the way: costume, words related to sheep breeding, wool processing, fur trade, pottery, the interior of the dwelling (with benches, strips of carpets, icons, and the dowry chest), – all are Romanian; it is only the creators of this vivid material culture, argues Kós Károly, that are not Romanians, as they make up "the most Eastern Magyar ethnic group" (p. 213). The author goes on to explain that the Romanian costume of the so-called Changos is justified by their poverty in Moldavia – although they are not poorer

aspect is not our principal area of interest, we will limit ourselves to a few references which present historical, as well as ethnographic interest.

Numerous scientific observers (historians, geographers) or simple travelers have signaled out in amazement that the Changos, whom they usually considered to be of Hungarian origin, hold to Romanian traditions and have preserved with tenacity their old Romanian costume from the Carpathian region.[2]

Sever Pop, the author of *Atlas lingvistic român* (*Romanian Linguistic Atlas*) (I), wrote the following: "The costume of the women in this region does not resemble that of the Hungarians; on the contrary, it presents all of the characteristics of the costume worn in the mountainous regions of Moldavia."[3]

---

here than in Transylvania (see I. Lupaş, *Studii istorice*, IV, Sibiu, 1944, p. 172) –, by their tendency of becoming a part of the Moldavian peasantry, and by the fact that their original costume was of a military type, of a "free Szeckler," and thus no longer justified beyond the Carpathians. That is why they started to make their clothes, although in Transylvania they had worn clothes made by craftsmen (pp. 199-200). The author does not make it clear from whom the Changos learned to quickly, here in Moldavia, to make Romanian clothes in a manner so different from the Moldavians' and why the Changos who remained in Transylvania wear or wore the Romanian costumes (see, for example, *Portul popular din judeţul Harghita*, Miercurea-Ciuc, 1979, pp. 129-166). The evidence used by the author, despite his intentions and conclusions, thoroughly prove the Romanian origin of this population).

[2](Editor's Note) Here is an earlier description of the costume worn by the Catholic inhabitants of the commune of Bărgăoani (in the county of Neamţ), a costume that was different from that of the old yeoman and of the other Romanians: "In the winter, men wear tight peasant trousers and shirts made of hempen cloth; most often, the sleeves of the shirts are emboidered at the bottom and dyed cotton threads are sewn on the collar. The married women wear white kerchiefs, and the girls are bare-headed. Maidens due to be married differ from the others in that they wear a wreath on their head and a lot of beads around their necks (Petru Condrea, "Geografia comunei Bârgăoani," in Societatea Geografică Română. Buletin, V, 1884, p. 69). See also a similar description in Cronica parohiei Barticeşti, VII, pp. 93-96, from where we learn that most men had

Often it has been said that the Changos are a Magyar people, mixed or pure, and, paradoxically, it has been noticed on numerous occasions that they wear only Romanian clothes. Nowhere has it been mentioned that a Chango dressed in Hungarian or Szeckler traditional costume. What determined these presumed Hungarians to wear the traditional Romanian costume specific to the mountain region? Some

---

long hair until 1920, and that girls used to dress up with strings of beads and necklaces made of silver coins.

Descriptions of the costumes worn by the Catholic Romanians in Moldavia can be found in: Iosif Petru M. Pal, op. cit.; Petru Râmneţeanu, *Die Absammung der Tsachangos*; P. Anton Bişoc, *Căsătoria*, Hălăuceşti, 1924; Alexandrina Enăchescu-Cantemir, *Portul popular românesc*, Craiova, 1937; Emilia Pavel, *Portul popular moldovenesc*, Iaşi, 1976; Wichmanné Herrman Júlia, "Moldvai csángó menyegzö Szabófalván" ("The Moldavian Wedding of the Changos at Săbăoani"), in *Ethnographia*, XLVII, 1936, no. 1-2, pp. 57-65; Domokos Pál Péter, op. cit., Mikecs Laszló, op. cit., Tancred Bănăţeanu, Gheorghe Focşa, Emilia Ionescu, *Arta populară in Republica Populară Română*, Bucureşti, 1957, maps 168-184 (here Eugen Nagy presents the Changos as a Magyar population, whose costume is very similar to the Romanian one, because their life is closely related to that of the Romanian people; he does not mention the Romanian language at all, and the words referring to costume are written in Hungarian orthography: keptár, kozsok, bernécz, szurtuk, flanyela etc.); Dr. Kós Károly, Szentimrei Judit, Dr. Nagy Jenö, op. cit.; Elena Secoşan, Paul Petrescu, *Portul popular de sărbătoare din România*, Bucureşti, 1984 (with a grave error about their native language and a true statement: "The Changos wear the Romanian costume, being loyal keepers of the ancient clothing customs of the Moldavian peasants," p. 127).

[3]See the review in Jryö Wichmanns, "Wörterbuch des ungarischen Moldauer Nordcsángo und des Hétfaluer Csángodialektes nebst Grammatikalischen Aufzeichnungen und Texten aus dem Nordesángódialekt," Helsinki, 1936, in *Bulletin linguistique*, VIII, 1940, p. 175. (Editor's Note: See also O.G. Lecca, *Dicţionar istoric, arheologic şi geografic*, Bucureşti, 1937, p. 137: "...what is more characteristic is that women wear the Romanian costume without exception." Unfortunately, this mention is made after a series of inaccurate observations.

Because of what he saw at the fair, on Easter (Brad, 1880), Ion Ionescu de la Brad writes that: "Most Orthodox Romanian women wore dresses, skirts, and long coats, only the Catholic Romanian women were dressed in the Romanian national costume" (See Constantin C. Diculescu, op. cit., p. 360).

attribute the fact to their recent assimilation by the Moldavian Romanians. But Petru Zöld noted already in the eighteenth century that they were wearing "Wallachian clothes, cheap, made by their wives." It is obvious that the Changos of those times, recently settled in Moldavia, had not had the necessary time to borrow the costume from the Moldavians, but that they had arrived with it from Transylvania.

Nicolae Iorga's opinion seems to be closest to the truth, as he admiringly manifests his surprise concerning the Romanian clothing of the Changos, whose women cover their heads "with big white shawls, very similar in their size and the way they are fastened to those worn by Romanian daughters and wives in the Făgăraş Mountains."[4] There is no wonder that their costume is similar to the one in the Făgăraş region, because they are of Transylvanian origin; the final commentary of the historian is not surprising either: "But these Hungarians, without being entirely Romanians, are far from being the foreigners that one might believe them to be."[5] The keen intuition of the historian sensed that something had happened behind the scenes of history, a process at that time not yet studied, which explains their Romanian costume.

An expert in the process of Szecklerization of the Romanians, G. Popa-Lisseanu is even more explicit, with the specification that he sees a similitude between the Szecklers and the Changos: "In the case of the Szecklers, as well as of the Changos, it is not only a matter of a

---

[4]Vasile Alecsandri, who knew very well the Catholic inhabitants of Mirceşti and its surroundings, wrote in one of his poems: *Bătrâni cu feţe stinse, români cu plete albe/Românce cu ochi negri şi cu ştergare albe* (Old men with withered faces, Romanians with white locks/Dark-eyed Romanian women wearing white headkerchiefs), referring to their women, because at that time in that region only they were wearing white headkerchiefs. Starting from the picturesque of the traditional costume, the artistic vision, helped by the intuition of the poet, formulates in verse a historical truth, which the science of language is trying to confirm only in our today.

[5]Nicolae Iorga, *România* cum *era până la 1918,* II, pp. 180-181

fortuitous Romanian influence, but one can say that it is a matter of a Romanian base, to which only modifications of detail were brought."[6] The two populations are however completely different, the only thing they had in common being a temporary historical symbiosis. Therefore, the Romanian base of many Szecklers cannot be identical, in its structure and dimension, with the Romanian base of the Changos, which differs in profoundness, in the way it is expressed, in all its spiritual and material aspects, and in its potential for development.

The impressions of a Hungarian observer are revealing. In 1887, Aladar Ballagi, the president of the Hungarian Geographic Society, visiting the village of Cleja (in the county of Bacău), could not conceal the first impression that its inhabitants made on him: "At first sight they look like Wallachians. Not only their costume, but also their physiognomy has a Wallachian imprint."[7] Although Ballagi had come to Cleja with a preconceived opinion, like most of the authors of those times, nevertheless, his first impression could not deceive him: their costume, their way of life, and their physiognomy are Romanian. But, like Bernát Munkácsi, he explained the phenomenon with the help of a strange hypothesis: he saw in them a species of degenerate Hungarians, mixed with Wallachians, from whom they would have borrowed Romanian characteristics. Historically, the supposition has

---

[6] G. Popa-Lisseanu, *op. cit.*, p. 115. (Editor's Note: The same observation, concerning the Romanian character of their art, is made by Coriolan Petranu, "Influence de l'art populaire des Roumains sur les autres peuples de Roumanie et sur les peuples voisins," in *Revue de Transylvanie*, II, 1936, no. 3, March, p. 320).

[7] *Les Hongrois en Moldavie*, p. 216 (Editor's Note: Here is the text from *Abrégé du Bulletin de la Societé Hongroise de Géographie*, Budapest, XVI, 1888, no. 1-2, pp. 1-2: Au premier abord, ils paraissent être Roumains Non seulement leurs vêtements, mais aussi leurs traits portent Pempreinte roumaine. The same author refers to the Chango mayor in Cleja, who used to recount passionately his feats at Plevna).

no foundation, because there are no Hungarian ethnographic elements known in their past.

Here are the findings of another foreign observer, this time a Frenchman, Count d'Hauterive, who came to Moldavia as secretary to Prince Alexandru Mavrocordat. In 1787, he noted in his memorial that the Catholic "Hungarians" in Moldavia are passionate and skillful dancers of Romanian dances: *Infatigables pour la danse, comme pour le travail, ils donnent au braule moldave une vivacité, qui le corrige de sa monotonie naturelle.*[8]

Today it is easy for us to understand why the "Hungarians" in Moldavia wore Romanian clothes, spoke Romanian, and danced passionately Romanian dances. The Frenchman, however, did not have any information regarding their Transylvanian Romanian antecedents. Nevertheless, he noted that the so-called "Hungarians" were dancing the Romanian *brâul*, and not the *ceardaş* or other Hungarian dances.

Another observation of the count deserves to be emphasized here: "Tireless at dance as well as at work." Their folklore tells about their passion for dancing: *Foaii vergi gi trifoi,/ Asă-I zocu-n sat la noi:/ Sî-nvârcesci căci doi,/ Sî-năinci, sî-napoi.* Today they are still known as very hard-working people and good farmers.[9] A beautiful quatrain says that the hardworking man does not return from the field at night, but sleeps there to make headway in the coolness of the next morning.

---

[8]Contele d'Hauterive, *Memoriu asupra* vechei *şi actualei stări a Moldovei,* Bucureşti, 1902, pp. 90-91; *braule, brâul.*

[9](Editor's Note) From among the many testimonies concerning their industriousness, worth mentioning is that provided by Professor Ion Simionescu, former president of the Romanian Academy: "Hardworking householders and farmers, the Changos live in harmony with the Romanians, who never did them any harm that would have reminded them of the fate met by the Romanians living among the Szecklers" (*Ţara noastră,* ed. II, Bucureşti, 1938, p. 289).

Fisoru cari-i fisor/ Hoginesci pi ogor;/ Nu sî culcî noaptea-n ţol,/ Doarmi pi pământu gol.

As for how long they had been in Moldavia, Count d'Hauterive registered the popular Moldavian tradition of those times, according to which these "Hungarians" would have come there in the time of Stephen the Great and then would have acquire the language and customs of the country. One thing is certain: the "Hungarians" about whom the author speaks represented, in their great majority, the recently immigrated Romanian population from Transylvania, established in Moldavia after 1700.

* * *

The historical destiny of the Changos was difficult. For a long time they were submitted to a process of Szecklerization and incorporation into the Magyar-Szeckler dominant nation. It goes without saying that the Hungarian historians of the past could recognize and interpret this process only in conformity with their historical doctrine, and with the national and political interests of the Hungarian state of that time. The history of the Changos was adjusted and presented in such a way as to correspond to those interests.

Fortunately, their true history was not completely lost, but was preserved in the form of the dialect still spoken by many of them today. A truly authentic document from their historical past, preserved in its wholeness as the language of their home (*Heimsprache*). It reflects in an objective manner the history and spirit of its speakers. The deciphering of the true history of the origins of the Changos can only be realized through a careful analysis of their Romanian dialect.

This study tries to carry out this task. The outline of their historical past presented here is only a beginning. Further study is needed to write the history of this population. It is important, however, that we have signaled out, for the first time, the existence and the historical significance of the Romanian dialect of this population, a dialect which substantiates the theory of their Romanian origin. This presentation, concise as it may be, we hope will serve in the future as a basis for discussion and a starting point for more elaborate studies.

Part II
Linguistic Aspects

Chapter 12

The Two Linguistic Aspects of the Chango Phenomenon

The Chango linguistic phenomenon involves two diverging aspects, effects of separate, distinct historical moments, both of an incontestable scholarly interest:

a) the original Transylvanian Romanian aspect;

b) the Hungarian aspect, a result of the process of Szecklerization.

Paying attention to only one of these two aspects, to the detriment of the other, is what has hindered all research in the past,[1] the inevitable result being that it was impossible to elucidate the problem of the origin of the Changos, despite all the efforts made by scholars. Only the Hungarian aspect of the problem was studied, while the original Romanian aspect was ignored or brushed aside.

---

[1] Szarvas Gábor, "A moldvai csángó nyelvről" ("About the Chango Language in Moldavia"), in *Magyar nyelvör*, Budapest, III, 1874, pp. 1-6; 49-54; Munkacsi Bernat, "A moldvai csángók nyelvjárása" ("About the Dialect of the Changos in Moldavia"), ibidem, IX, 1880, pp. 444-455; 481-493; 529-233; X, 1881, pp. 1-6; 49-54; 101-107; 149-158; 199-205 (in 1881, under the title "A csángó nyelvöl"); Rubinyi Mozes, "Adalékok a moldvai csángó nyelvjárásáhos" ("Contributions Regarding the Dialect of the Changos in Moldavia"), ibidem, XXX, 1901, pp. 57-65; 1901, pp. 57-65; 190-116; 170-182; 227-235; XXXI, 1902, pp. 1-7; 82-87; 143-148; 202-208 (in 1902, under the title "Ujabb adalékok a csángók nyelvjéréséhoz").

At the same time, Romanian scholars considered the problem of the Changos in Moldavia to be of foreign origin, namely Magyar, and they felt that the subject belonged in the area of interest and research of Hungarian scholars. Consequently, they did not pay attention to the Romanian dialect spoken by the Changos, in which without a previous analysis of the linguistic facts, they saw only the faulty dialect of an allogenous population, which would have only recently acquired the Romanian language. They forgot, or did not know, that during the process of Szecklerization most of the so-called Changos did not abandon their old Transylvanian dialect, but continued to speak it with their families and thus, when they emigrated, they brought it with them to Moldavia in the eighteenth century. After they had established themselves in their new homeland, most of them abandoned and quickly forgot their adopted Hungarian language, continuing to speak only Romanian in their traditional dialect.

How do we know these things? One substantial proof is that they speak the same dialect today.

The Romanian-Hungarian bilingualism in some villages and their Catholic religion were not of a nature to stimulate the scholarly curiosity of Romanian researchers. Thus, the Transylvanian Romanian dialect, the oldest linguistic expression of this population, remained unknown to scholars.

Based on a series of new historical-linguistic grounds, in this part we intend to demonstrate that the Romanian dialect of the Changos was spoken for centuries in Transylvania, that the problems raised by this dialect are not at all of a lesser importance than the problems raised by other Romanian dialects, but on the contrary, they can be of interest to Romanian historians and linguists, even if, for one reason or another, the scholars of the past did not study it.

Chapter 13

The Sibilant Character
of the Chango Dialect

The Romanian Chango dialect is part of the almost forgotten category of sibilant Transylvanian dialects, which covered a larger area in the past than today. While the rhotacistic Transylvanian dialects were of much interest to the scholars and were studied by many Romanian and foreign linguists, so that this problem was, in broad outline, elucidated, the sibilant dialects, most of which disappeared before the appearance of dialectology as a science, remained almost unnoticed by the scholars.

These dialects could be divided in two principal groups:

a) The southwestern group, extended throughout southwestern Transylvania, the Banat, and northwestern Oltenia, where the sibilant pronunciation, although in a phase of disappearing, can still be heard today;

b) The group in southeastern Transylvania, represented today by the dialect of the Changos in Moldavia, who emigrated here in the eighteenth century.

The first one to point out the phenomenon of the sibilant pronunciation in southeastern Transylvania was the folklorist Enea Hodoş, in the preface to his collection of folk poetry published in

1892.[1] This phenomenon was later put into scholarly circulation by G. Weigand, in his study dealing with the communities with /s/.[2]

As far as the group in southeastern Transylvania is concerned, there are a series of attestations that illustrate the history of the sibilant dialect in this region.

We know that the Szecklers were colonized here in the twelfth and thirteenth centuries as guardians and defenders of the eastern border of the Hungarian kingdom.[3] By force of circumstances, the Szeckler colonists had no choice but to come into contact with the Romanians and to borrow some words from their language, especially toponyms.[4] For example, they borrowed from them the toponym *Kászon,* attested to in documents more than once in the fourteenth century, which reproduces the Romanian *Casân,* in sibilant pronunciation, the way the Changos pronounce it today. About this borrowing, N. Drăganu specifies that "the Hungarian *Kászon* is nothing but the normal Hungarian evolution of *Caşin,* with the /sz/ pronunciation of /ş/ usual for some Szecklers and Changos."[5] The case is not that, however, of a "normal Hungarian evolution of *Caşin*" as far as /sz/ for /ş/ is concerned, but that the Hungarian form *Kászon* produces the Romanian sibilant pronunciation of *Casân* of a

---

[1]Enea Hodoş, *Poezii populare din Bănat,* Caransebeş, 1892, p. 5.

[2]Gustav Weigand, "Der Ursprung der s-Gemeinden," in *Neunter Jahreschericht...,* 1902, pp. 113-137.

[3]G. Popa-Lisseanu, *Secuii şi secuizarea românilor,* pp. 33-39, 53-56; Sabin Opreanu, *Ţinutul secuilor: Contribuţii de geografie umană şi de etnografie,* Cluj, 1928, pp. 58-59.

[4]Teodor Chindea, *Contribuţii la istoria românilor din Ciurgeul Ciucului,* Gheorghieni, 1930, pp. 21-25.

[5]N. Drăganu, *Românii în veacurile IX-XIV pe baza toponimiei şi a onomasticei,* Bucureşti, 1933, pp. 542-543.

population that lived in south-eastern Transylvania and spoke Romanian in a sibilant dialect.[6]

While studying the present Szeckler population in the region around the town of Târgu Secuiesc, the Hungarian scholar Géza Bakó observed: "Certainly, the present population of this region is no longer a Chango one, but the infiltration of some Chango dialectal elements in the language of the Szecklers in this region shows that the Szecklers found here and assimilated an important number of speakers of the Chango dialect."[7]

"…found here and assimilated…" The conclusion of the author appears natural and logical. Therefore, in a chronological order, the problem of the relations between the medieval Szecklers and "Changos" presents itself as follows, according to Géza Bakó:

a) When they settled in southeastern Transylvania, the Szecklers found there an older, native population, with whom they established peaceful relations of cohabitation, a population which the author calls Changos. The linguistic facts show that in the region of Târgu Secuiesc there lived in the past a Chango, native population, anterior to the Szecklers.

b) In time, the Szecklers, who held political power, assimilated an important number of the speakers of the sibilant Chango dialect. Therefore, the Szecklers were the assimilators and the Changos were assimilated natives.

---

[6](Editor's Note) Even today, the toponym is pronounced Casin in the language of the local Romanian population. "The Casin Valley includes five localities: Plăieşii de Jos, Plăieşii de Sus, Imper, Iacobeni, and Casinul Nou" (Nicolae Dunăre, "Raporturi interetnice în Valea Casinului," in *Almanahul Muzeului din Cristu Secuiesc*, 1971, p. 370).

[7]Bakó Géza, op. cit., p. 39.

c) In this process of assimilation, some Chango dialectal elements, including the sibilant pronunciation, penetrated into the language of the Szecklers in this region and have remained until today.

The following question arises: who were these native inhabitants, those Changos who spoke in a sibilant dialect? Obviously, if the Szecklers assimilated a great number of the speakers of this dialect, it means that they could not have been either Szecklers or Magyars, because in that case there would have been no assimilation. Then who were they, what was their nationality? They could not have been anything else but the native inhabitants of that region, from whom the Szecklers borrowed the toponym *Kászon,* with the local sibilant pronunciation (*Casân*). Therefore, they were Romanians speaking a sibilant dialect. After their assimilation by the Szecklers, the old sibilant pronunciation began to enter into the adopted Szeckler language, as a reflex of the Romanian stratum over the Szeckler superstratum.

It is necessary that we specify that the pronunciation /s/:/ş/ (/sz/:/s/) is neither of Szeckler nor Hungarian origin. It entered the language of the Szecklers from the language of the assimilated population, namely from the Romanian language. At that time these people were not yet known by the name of Changos, which would later be given to them by the Szecklers. The sibilant pronunciation is specific only to the Changos, being unknown to the Hungarian and Szeckler phonetical tradition. Every time is appears in a regional Hungarian dialect, the case is that of a non-Magyar phonetical phenomenon, which entered the language as a result of the assimilation of foreigners, in this case of the Romanian native population which pronounced *Casân*. This Romanian toponym and its Hungarian version *Kászon* represent widely circulated examples, documenting that during the fourteenth century and certainly earlier the pronunciation with /s/ was a traditional phonetical element in the language of the Romanians of southeastern Transylvania.

1. Even today some Szeckler inhabitants of the town of Vlăhiţa have family names with sibilant pronunciation (*Minisz, Kozán*) inherited from their Romanian ancestors.[8] In other words, the ancestors of the Szeckler population of this region were Romanians, who, before Szecklerization, were speaking Romanian in a sibilant dialect. After their total linguistic Szecklerization this pronunciation began to disappear in their adopted language, being maintained, however, in the two old Romanian names (*Minis, Cozan : Miniş, Cojan*).

2. From *Codex Bandinus* (1646) we learn that some Catholic inhabitants of the localities Valea Seacă, Stăneşti, and Cotnari had Romanian family names pronounced sibilantly (*Kozokar; Kozan*).[9] Those who had these names were originally from Transylvania, from the regions with Romanian sibilant pronunciation. From this onomastic data it results that in the seventeenth century the Transylvanian sibilant pronunciation also began to infiltrate on the other side of the Carpathians, in Moldavia.

3. In the Romanian-Italian conversation textbook entitled *Diverse materie in lingua moldava,* written by the missionary Antonio Mauro sometime around 1760,[10] the presence of the sibilant dialect among the Catholic inhabitants of Răchiteni (in the region of Roman), where the author was rector, can be noticed. The missionary knew the Romanian language very well and, as a rule, avoided the forms that had a strong dialectal character. However, under the influence of his parishioners,

---

[8]Sabin Opreanu, op. cit., p. 71.

[9]V.A. Urechia, *Codex Bandinus*, pp. 105, 112, 125.

[10]Carlo Tagliavini, "Alcuni monoscritti sconosciuti di missionary cattolici italiani in Moldavia," (the eighteenth century), in *Studii rumeni,* IV, 1929-1930, pp. 51-104.

he adopted certain sibilant pronunciations, for example: *mossa*, for *moasă* (*moaşa* = midwife), *crisma*, for *crâsma* (*crâşmă* = tavern), *rosigna* (verb), for *rusâna* (*ruşina* = to be ashamed), *enselatoare*, for *înselătoare* (*înşelătoare* = deceiving), *slusba*, for *sluzba* (slujba = sermon), *lenes, ispasim, akusa*, etc.

4. Therefore, the parishioners of the missionary Mauro, who had only recently arrived from Transylvania, were speaking in their traditional sibilant dialect, with specific phonetical phenomena (/ş/ : /s/ and /z/ : /j/).

5. In the manuscript from Miclăuşeni, written at the beginning of the nineteenth century in the Cyrillic alphabet, we find eight popular medical recipes, written in the local dialect, with titles like: *di săli, di trânzi* (*de sale* = for the loins; *de trănji* = for hemorrhoids).[11] Therefore, at the beginning of the nineteenth century, the Changos of the northern group continued to speak in their old Transylvanian dialect, as many of them still do today.[12]

---

[11]Epifanie Cozarescu, "Un manuscript de folklore medical des alentours de Roman (en Roumanie)," in *XXII-e Congrés international d'histoire de la medicine. Compte rendu*, Bucarest, 1970, pp. 135-136 (Editor's Note: The manuscript belongs to the Sturdza library (Miclăuşeni) and is kept in Roman. The form trinzi is also attested in Apostolul de la Braşov (a Moldavian copy dating from the seventeenth century, with "a marked Catholic influence"): "And Poplie's father was suffering from typhoid fever and water trindzi" (see Valeria Căliman, "Instituţii şi realităţi medieval româneşti atestate în lexical de la Braşov," in *Cumidava*, III, 1969, p. 408).

[12](Editor's Note) We add the following: The scrivener of Neculce's chronicle, in sibilant writing, who "could not be but a Chango, whose native tongue was Romanian" (see Liviu Onu, *The Critic of the Texts and the Editing of the Old Romanian Literature*, Bucharest, 1973, pp. 351-356; with bibliography for the sibilant uttering). In the registry of the Hălăuceşti Catholic church, which began in 1780, the missionaries often registered the name of the parishioner according to their pronunciation. Thus: Cupkilas instead of Copilaş and Bisoc (written by the Italian missionaries) or Biszok (written by the Hungarians) instead of Bişoc (see The Chronicle of the Barticeşti Church, I, pp. 8-9). In status animarum of the Barticeşti

* * *

From what we have seen so far, the documents establish that the sibilant dialect is an old Romanian regional dialect, spoken by the Romanian population in southeastern Transylvania ever since the twelfth-thirteenth centuries, a population which later was more or less Szecklerized and part of which emigrated to Moldavia. Consequently, the dialect of the Moldavian Changos does not represent, as some thought, a degraded dialect, recently created by a foreign population that could not pronounce the sounds of the Romanian language.

The uninterrupted historical continuity of this sibilant dialect, from the twelfth and thirteenth centuries until today, demonstrates its ancientness, as well as Transylvanian Romanian belonging of its speakers.

This Romanian dialect is one of the oldest Transylvanian regional dialects, which has been preserved in its archaic phonetical phase. What were the historical causes that favored this fact?

The geographic isolation in which the predecessors of the Changos lived for centuries in the region of the Eastern Carpathians in the depressions of Ciuc and Giurgeu, far from great lines of communication, explains, according to the principles of linguistic geography, the prolonged preservation of this dialect. A series of other historical causes added to this. as a consequence of the process of religious and linguistic Szecklerization, the Szecklerized Catholic Romanians isolated themselves from their Orthodox conationals. Because at that time religious differentiation interposed as a powerful isolating factor, their Romanian dialect became little by little a separate dialectal area, which participated less or not at all in the

---

branch in 1786, there is registered Zittar (instead of Jitaru) Ioan with his wife Ana (ibidem, p. 92).

linguistic changes that would occur in other dialects. When, in a more recent period, the archaic pronunciation disappeared from the language of the Romanians in southeastern Transylvania, it was still maintained in the separate area of the dialect of the Szecklerized Catholic Romanians. After their emigration to Moldavia, the same religious difference again favored their linguistic isolation. Like their Romanian costume, their sibilant dialect was still maintained here with tenacity, as a distinctive sign of their religious belonging.

Asă sî grăiesci la noi la catolis ("This is how we Catholics speak"), some old speakers will say, to explain the differences in pronunciation in comparison with the Moldavian dialect.

Nowadays, due to frequent contacts with the Moldavians, this dialect has been slowly integrating into the Moldavian dialect, and together with it, into the common literary Romanian language. But the old speakers, especially the women, have not given it up.

As one can see, the study of the old Romanian Chango dialect can be useful for the study of the history of the Romanian language as a whole, confirming the truth that, for reconstructing the stages of the language previous to the sixteenth century, "even the most insignificant – in semblance – regional dialect can be of use."[13]

Another example, this time interesting for the whole Romance space, is the preservation in this dialect of the term of kinship *ler, lerule, leru-neu,* meaning "brother-in-law,"[14] which proves that the

---

[13]Emil Petrovici, *Studii de dialectologie şi toponimie*, Bucureşti, 1970, p. 104.

[14](Editor's Note) The related term *ler* is known by us, as well as by the author since his childhood. The only written attestation, unknown to dialectologists, can be found in the possession of Priest Ath. Vasilescu, Monografia mănăstirei şi comunei Doljeşti din judeţul Roman, Roman, 1930, in a text which is rendered in a less authentic way, railing at the Catholic Romanians' manner of speaking (the author himself, despite his unusual confessionalism, uses this term sometimes) from the villages belonging to this commune (Buhonca, Buruieneşti, and Rotunda): "Evening. Several villagers are

term, although it has disappeared from the Romanian language today, must have circulated in the Daco-Romanian language, which would explain, perhaps, the toponym *Lereşti* (in the county of Argeş) and the family names *Lerescu, Lereanu.* This term of Latin origin (<Lat. *cognatus*), but it was maintained in the dialectal variant of the Changos. Attested as a term of kinship in Justinian's *Digestele,*[15] it was not preserved in any Romance language. It disappeared from Romanian as well, but we still find it today in the Romanian dialect of the Changos. Consequently, we considered that the study of this dialect would be of interest for Romanian linguistics, although approaching, after almost a century of Romanian dialectology, an unknown dialect, especially the dialect of the Changos, usually considered of Hungarian origin, might appear as a venturesome attempt. Prestigious scholarly works, like Gustav Weigand's linguistic atlas and *Atlasul limbii române* (*The Atlas of the Romanian Language*), do not register this regional dialect. Famous Hungarian linguists, like Gábor Szarvas and Moózes Rubinyi, were convinced that the Changos had learned to speak Romanian from the Moldavians. Without examining the evidence put forward and its argumentation, this thesis was also considered the Hungarian linguists the only incontestable specialists on this problem. That is why the majority of

---

gathered in the middle of the road and have a discussion. A woman passes by and, instead of good evening, she greets them this way: 'Are you still discussing?' One of them answers: "We're just having a rest.' Here is the discussion between them: 'Listen, Ioză! I met your ler (brother-in-law) yesterday, and he told me that he was heading for the fair in Suboani (Săbăoani)."' The text, explained by the author in parenthesis, continues with the ironical repetition of the word ceala, which in this idiom often appears instead of verbs (pp. 195-196). Worth mentioning are the phrase ci fel gi (ce fel de = what kind of) and two rare words: cintru (half), pruzesti (you joke). Rectifications: ler-tu (your brother-in-law); Sâboani, with two syllables, not Suboani.

[15]See *infra,* pp. 90-92.

Romanian historical, linguistic, and geographical studies present the so-called Changos as a Hungarian population.[16]

Iosif M. Pál and Petru Râmneanţu are the only ones who, using different criteria for their research, assert explicitly the Romanian origin of the Changos. Starting from historical-ethnographic or biological premises, helped by their intuition, the two scholars reached the conclusion that from an ethnic standpoint this population belongs to the Romanian nation. If, at that time, the linguists had also studied the Romanian dialect of this population, this conclusion would have become a scholarly certainty. The information we have today regarding this original Romanian dialect have considerably enlarged our scholarly horizons and opened new perspectives concerning this controversial problem.

---

[16]Just one example: George Ioan Lahovari, C.I. Brătianu, and Grigore G. Tocilescu, *Marele dictionar geografie al României,* I-V, Bucureşti, 1898-1902, in which the population of the Catholic villages in Moldavia is considered to be of Hungarian origin.

Chapter 14

Gábor Szarvas's Research on the Dialect of the Changos

Gábor Szarvas was the first scholarly researcher of the Hungarian Chango dialect. His contribution would have been much improved had he extended his research to include also the Romanian dialect spoken by the great majority of the Changos. In this case, he would have been able to establish a series of phonetical interferences between the two dialects, the Romanian and the Hungarian, which would have led them to some very important conclusions from a historical and linguistic point of view. Unfortunately, things did not happen this way, and so the "enigma" of the Chango phenomenon remained unsolved.

Although he was an erudite and experienced linguist, Gábos Szarvas's findings were limited. Completely Romanianized as far as their costume and customs are concerned, he found, this population is to a great extent Romanianized from a linguistic standpoint in the northern part and is bilingual in the southern part, where all the men speak both Hungarian and Romanian.[1] About the Romanian dialect he gives no information; but, analyzing the phonetical characteristics of the Hungarian dialect, he immediately becomes convinced that the Changos pronounce the vowels of this dialect in a very peculiar way.

---

[1]Szarvas Gábor, *op. cit.,* p. 1.

And with good reason, because anyone who knows this dialect realizes that its phonetical system is different from that of Hungarian. The Changos cannot pronounce the typical Hungarian vowels, /a/, /é/, /ö/, /ō/, /ü/, /û/ which they avoid or replace with other vowels. The word *füstös* (smoked) is pronounced *fisztësz* (*fistas*) in their dialect. The Hungarian sibilant /s/ (Romanian /ş/) is pronounced /sz/ (Rom. /s/), according to the old sibilant Romanian pronunciation. The dental consonant /t/, followed by the vowels /i/, /y/ is pronounced /cs/ (Rom. /c/). What is the cause of this pronunciation? There is only one explanation: all of these sounds, strange to the ears of Hungarians, are derived from Romanian phonetics, and are neutral to the ears of Romanians, later called Changos, acquired the Hungarian language but could not get accustomed to its phonetical system of a Finno-Ugric type, replacing it with that of their Romanian language. This is how a mixed Hungarian dialect came into being, called by the Szecklers *csángó*, which Szarvas studied without examining at all the Romanian dialect of the Changos whom he considered "Romanianized". Perhaps the Hungarian linguist did not even know Romanian, or knew very little, and so much the less the Romanian dialects. This would explain but not justify his error, which misled so many generations of Hungarian scholars, who remained under the mistaken conviction that the Changos were genuine Hungarians, who had learned Romanian from the Moldavians. He did not know or did not want to use the notion of Szecklerized Romanians.

It goes without saying that in his country the conclusion of this linguist was considered the last word of scholarship. At that age of knowledge there was no one, either in Romania or abroad, to present the state of facts and to correct his errors. Officially and theoretically, the whole historical evolution of the Changos was misrepresented, inverted: from Romanians Szecklerized in Transylvania, they came to be presented as Hungarians Romanianized in Moldavia. The process of Szecklerization was transformed into a process of Romanianization. This way the thesis regarding the Hungarian origin of the Changos was adopted by most of the Hungarian historians and journalists and taken over as an axiom by many Romanian authors.[2]

This error is also made by Sever Pop, one of the most distinguished Romanian dialectologists. Conforming to the general opinion regarding the Changos, the linguist from Cluj wrote the following about their costume and language: Par leur costume et leur manière de parler ils sont entièrement assimilés aux Roumains.[3] Thus, the original Romanian basis of this population is interpreted as a

---

[2]Mikecs László, *op. cit.*, pp. 330-399, points out 242 titles of studies dealing with the Changos, written mostly by Hungarian authors. None of them deals with their Romanian dialect. Since 1941 the number of these works has increased considerably.

[3]Sever Pop, op. cit., p. 178 (Editor's Note: During his researches for ALR, Sever Pop did not examine the Romanian language in any Moldavian Catholic village. The explanation of this can be found, indirectly, in the introduction to *Micul atlas linguistic român*, part I, vol. I, Cluj, 1938: "I chose the communes for each county after conferring with the administrative and school authorities in the capital of each county. I avoided the communes which had been founded last century, with a population which had come here from the surrounding areas or from more distant regions" (p. 11). The quote reproduced by Mărtinaş refers to the bilingual Changos, those speaking Romanian being regarded as Romanians, unlike the author who glossed the dictionary: "Wichmanns admits that many villages inhabited by Changos were made Romanian, but it seems to us that he is wrong when stating that nur der ungarishe Name des Dorfes, die katolische Konfessoin, die Frauentracht und die Benennung 'Ungur' zeugten noch von ihren fruheren Csangotum" (p. VII), for "indeed, the Hungarian name of a village, the women's costume, and the appellation of Hungarian does not necessarily imply the Hungarian origin of a village which is Romanian today. The women's regional costume has nothing Hungarian about it; on the contrary, it evinces almost all the characteristics of the Romanian costume from the mountainous regions of Moldavia... The name Hungarian was part of a Romanian tradition in Moldavia and it designated the Romanians who had arrived from Transylvania" (pp. 175-176). As far as the Catholic religion is concerned, Sever Pop had in mind "a late remnant of this confession, which was earlier represented by the Cuman bishopric," also mentioning the letter sent by Pope Gregory IX in 1234 (p. 176).

consequence of assimilation. The error can be explained through the fact that, in this matter, Romanian scholarship has lagged behind Hungarian scholarship. It could also be partly due to the limiting of his research only to surface aspects, because many Changos, especially the young ones, who speak the Moldavian dialect very well, conceal their own dialect in front of the strangers, because they make fun and laugh at their "lisping" speech.

In connection with the "concealing" of their dialect, I have an older experience, of a different nature, with the Chango students in the Szeckler region. Sometime in the years 1926-1930, some of these students from the Roman-Catholic high-school in Târgu Mureş would give very poor answers or no answers at all in the Romanian language class, saying that they did not understand, that they did not know Romanian. I took this into account and consequently I offered these students special attention. But with all our efforts, despite our minimum requirements, no progress was being made. Until one day, one of the Szeckler students, seeing the uselessness of our efforts and tired of this comedy, gave his Chango colleague away, saying:

"Sir, he knows Romanian, 'cause they (the Changos) speak Romanian at home." And he provoked him, addressing him in Hungarian:

"Tell the truth, don't you speak Romanian at home with your grandma? I heard you! Tell the truth!"

Then he said to me: "He knows Romanian, sir, but he pretends that he doesn't know, and you are wasting your time with him."

Irritated, I thought it was a schoolboy prank in bad taste, which could not go unpunished. But the usual failing grade did not seem to be the best solution. I suspected that this prank had to have a hidden meaning. During a break I took the boy aside and he finally admitted his guilt:

"I know Romanian, sir. I lied when I said I didn't, and I ask you to forgive me... But this is how it is with us, I don't know how to say it, how to explain to you."

And the student hesitated, kept silent. Then, little by little, I understood that some Chango students pretended to be Szecklers and that they did not know any Romanian, not to be suspected and accused by their Szeckler colleagues that, because they spoke Romanian very well, they had remained Romanians in their souls. So that the boys were trying in very way to prove that they were Szecklers in their "soul" as well, that is why they pretended not to know Romanian. Then I understood...

From this tragic human comedy, a mirror of the period, as from other situations, I understood that some of the Changos in the Szeckler region although Szecklerized still spoke Romanian at home. The honest retort of the Szeckler student remained imprinted on my mind: "they speak Romanian at home..."

Chapter 15

The Transylvanian-Moldavian Phonetical Dualism

While Hungarian linguists have studied exclusively the problem of the Hungarian dialect (spoken by a minority of Changos), our intention is to study the Romanian dialect (spoken by their great majority). In order to verify the validity of past research about the Changos and to establish how they speak today, between the years 1950 and 1970 we made linguistic investigations in the following villages: Gherăeşti, Hălăuceşti, Barticeşti, Săbăoani, Pildeşti, Răchiteni, Butea, Fărcăşeni, Oţeleni, Sagna, Buruieneşti, Rotunda, Adjudeni, and Tămăşeni (of the northern group), Prăjeşti, Văleni, Mărgineni, Luizi-Călugăra, Valea Seacă, Valea Mare, Lespezi, Dărmăneşti, and Faraoani (of the southern group).

Faced with so many versions, opinions, and contradictory hypotheses concerning the Changos which circulate both in Hungarian and in Romanian specialized literature, the purpose of our investigations was threefold:

a) to establish, based on facts, whether they maintain their own separate Romanian dialect, different from the Moldavian one;

b) if such a dialect still exist today, to establish, using the same criterion, its prevalent phonetical characters;

c) to establish, scientifically, whether they represent a Magyar denationalized population assimilated by the Romanians (Gábor Szarvas's thesis) or are a population of Transylvanian Romanians, who went through the well-known process of Szecklerization.

The investigations were made especially in the villages of the northern group, where the Changos have lived far from any Szeckler influence, as opposed to the southern group, where contact with the Szecklers is still maintained, influencing their dialectal speech.

Consequently, the object of our investigations were the most characteristic phonetical peculiarities of their Romanian dialect and its phonetical system, in comparison with the same system in the Moldavian dialect. We did not insist on the phonetical aspects common to both the Moldavian and Transylvanian dialects, such as, for instance, the palatalization of the labial sounds.

In the bilingual villages, like Săbăoani, where part of the population speaks Hungarian, our observations included the phonetical system of this dialect as well, to identify the phonetical phenomena borrowed from the Romanian Chango dialect.

We also studied the lexical peculiarities of the dialect, especially certain archaisms of Latin origin, as well as some regionalisms of Transylvanian origin.

Finally, we studied certain elements of Chango folklore: fairy tales, carols, sayings, and proverbs.

We came into contact with people of all categories, gathering observations, linguistic facts, information, and opinions of the speakers. All of our conclusions were drawn from conversations with people who usually did not even suspect that they were being studied. When the informer chose to speak, becoming more communicative, we used the method of the indirect question: How do you call that thing? How do you pronounce that word? How do the old way (for example: *injăcţie* = injection), and the old people in a different way (*inzăcţie*)? Why is it that at home you speak with /s/, /z/ (for example *săd* = I sit, *cozoc* = sheepskin coat), and at the cultural center you do not speak this way (we noticed that the same person pronounced *şăd, cojoc*)? Who speaks more beautifully, you or the Moldavians?

The questions varied depending on the circumstances, and the answers varied from one person to another. But, when taken as a whole, we can understand the phonetical structure of this dialect, its progressive integration into the Moldavian dialect, and this important linguistic phenomenon: the dialectal dualism of the speakers. Depending on the different situations of communication, people use their own dialect with their family and in the relations among themselves, and the Moldavian dialect when they come in contact with strangers. We noticed the esteem that they have for the dialect of the Moldavians, who "speak more beautifully than us" (grăiesc mai frumos ca noi). Sometimes during the conversation some unusual words would be said (for example: polozănie, vintrisel), other times a rare expression (for example: nu ci mai nisăli atâta), for which we would ask for explanations. Other times, more rarely, an archaic sound would be heard: l'e sama, măi băieci (ia sama, măi băiete – be careful, boy), an echo from long ago.[1]

---

[1]One day I was with the family of an acquaintance in Săbăoani. At a certain moment a bottle of wine was brought to table, with the invitation: *L'e gi be, domnule, l'e gi be, nu ci-ngie* (*ia de bea, nu te-mbia* – come and drink). I answered the invitation, but this pronunciation seemed very strange to me. It was an old formula of invitation, used only when there were strangers at the table.

I asked: "Where did you hear these words, *l'e gi be?*"

"This is how we old people speak, but the young ones speak differently, in the new fashion: *poftiţi, serviţi!* The world changes, the language of people changes too."

The archaic sound *l'e*, with /l'/ (palatal), meaning *ie* (*ia* < *a lua* – to take), present in the language of some people who are said to be Hungarians and to have been assimilated recently by the Romanians, bewildered us. How did this man know such

In our investigations we appealed to the most valuable informants, to the old people, especially the uneducated women,[2] who preserve with tenacity the dialect of past generations. Under no circumstances will they deviate from tradition. *Asă-i la noi, alfeli nu cscim sî grăim, nu pucem* ("This is how we are, we do not know how to speak differently, we cannot"), women will say. Most of them speak in their dialect in any circumstances, because they did not learn the Moldavian dialect. If you manage to win their confidence, which can be difficult, they are excellent informants.

We also observed how the young people talk, to realize in what direction their dialect is evolving.

We also found that the folklore of this population is not extremely rich.[3] We did not find out remarkable things in the epic genre. What

---

an old pronunciation? The explanation was simple: "This is how we old people speak." Centuries ago, the Romanian language used the imperative *l'e* with /l'/ (palatal), then, sometime in the sixteenth-seventeenth centuries, the language evolved to the present regional form of pronunciation /ie/. But since then three centuries have passed. And our speaker in Săbăoani, presumed to be Hungarian, still uses the archaic form *l'e* of the medieval Dacian-Romanian. The problem that arises here is the following: how do the people in Săbăoani know to use the sound /l'/, according to the pronunciation of the Romanian language anterior to the sixteenth century, when this sound disappeared from the Moldavian dialect? It is clear that these people, who represent a new stratification of inhabitants settled here in the eighteenth century, did not receive the sound from the Moldavians, but brought it with them from their native land, Transylvania. Consequently, the presumed Hungarians are not Hungarians, but Transylvanian Romanians, who still preserve the old Dacian-Romanian pronunciation *l'eu, l'ei, l'e*. This sound is about to disappear, surviving only in a few villages.

[2]See Emil Petrovici, "Folelor de la moţii din Sărişoara," in *Anuarul Arhivei de Folelor,* V, 1939, p. 120: "Transylvanian folklore and authentic Transylvanian language can be gathered only from the women who live in Western Transylvania."

[3](Editor's Note) The author's research is not complete and his statement should be taken with a grain of salt. In reality, the Romanian folklore in these villages is rich, but no one has taken any interest in gathering it. a few bibliographical notes: Ath. Vasilescu, *op. cit.,* p. 152; two ballads (*Moşneagul* and *Toma Alimoş*), picked up from Teţcani (in the county of Neamţ) by M.V. Hordilă, in *Satul,* VIII, 1938, nr. 92-93, iul.

we heard were the stories known from school textbooks. Here and there some reminiscences, some stanzas from songs and tales that seem to have existed once. The folk songs that we heard were the usual ones in current circulation in the country. Only the carols proved to be older and full of vitality.

* * *

With regard to the phonetical dualism of the Changos in Moldavia, by which we understand that they use alternately the Transylvanian dialect and the Moldavian dialect, the main difficulty that scholars have to face is posed by the fact that, as we have already mentioned, they only speak in their own dialect with their family, friends, and people from the same village. If there is a stranger among them, they speak in the Moldavian dialect or as literary as possible. Especially the young people want to prove by all means how they learned the literary language in school.

To discover elements of their traditional dialect, the scholarly researcher must have a great deal of patience and take time to get close to the informants he is studying. The best solution is for him to live among them for a time, to be able in this way to observe the usage of this home dialect, very different from the Moldavian one.

The author who undertook his research also to verify a series of data that he possessed from his own linguistic experience, encountered a few difficulties. Avoiding to speak with those investigated anything but the literary language, he had to wait a long time until he heard in the home of his host for instance, Petre Agu in Buruieneşti, first with the women, pronunciations like *păreci* (for *păreti* – wall), *frunci* (for

---

–aug., p. 29, and nr. 96, nov., p. 18; a text used in Romanian village rites (*caloian* = rainmaker) and a carol, culled by Emil Apostol in Pildeşti (in the county of Neamţ), and a poem letter from Tămăşeni, in *Folelor din Moldova,* I, Bucureşti, 1969, pp. 243, 330, 513. Folk texts are also included in *Cronica parohiei Barticeşti,* VII.

frunti – forehead), *sococalî* (for *socoteali* – plan), *lapci* (for *lapti* – milk), unknown in the Moldavian dialect, but attested to, as is well-known, in the central and northern part of Transylvania and in the Banat. The same thing also happened with other families in Buruieneşti, and also in other villages, as we were to find out later.[4]

I noticed that, as I became more intimate with the people I was studying, my hosts preferred to avoid the sounds /ş/ and /j/, replacing them with /s/ and respectively /z/: *closcî* (for *cloşcî* = mother hen), sanţ (for *şanţ* = ditch), *săpci* (for *şăpci* = caps), *coazî* (for *coajî* = peel), *cozoc* (for *cojoc* = sheepskin coat), *grizî* (for *grijî* = worry), *zurnal* (for *jurnal* = journal), *baraz* (for *baraj* = dam). I was curious to question my informant about what I had noticed, so I asked him:

"Bade Agule, did you live in Transylvania?"

"No!" he answered.

"Did you live in the Banat or Oltenia?"

"No!"

"I see you pronounce the words as they do in Transylvania, in the Banat. For instance, I heard your wife saying *closca cu puisori* (with /s/), and you say *cloşca cu puişori* (with /ş/). Why this difference?"

The man explained to me in the Moldavian dialect:

"At home we speak differently, in the old way. With my wife and my mother I cannot even speak except the way they know how, like the old people did in the days of yore, as we, the Catholics used to speak a long time ago."

"But why don't you speak like that with me?"

"With you it's a different matter, you are not one of us. With you I speak differently, because if I speak like the old folks I'm afraid you will laugh at me. And besides, the language of the old people is not

---

[4](Editor's Note) See also Grigore Rusu, *Structura fonologică a graiurilor daco-române*, Bucureşti, 1983, p. 126.

even that beautiful, sir. They speak with /s/ and /z/, as the people in olden times, who were not educated. Now we have more schools, people talk more beautifully. The young ones laugh at the speech of the old folks, they don't like it anymore."[5]

As we can see, the man did not have a very good opinion about the old dialect which he spoke with his family and his fellow-villagers. Thus, he avoided to speak it in front of strangers out of embarrassment. With the latter he used the phonetical system of the Moldavian dialect, which seemed to him more beautiful. *Badea* Agu could pass from one pronunciation to the other very easily.

I chose my informants mostly from among the old people, especially women, because they represented the most conservative element in the matter of language. Their dialect, from the standpoint of its authenticity, is incomparably more valuable, more representative, than the dialect of the young people, who have adopted to a certain extent the Moldavian dialect.

The coexistence of two different phonetical systems in the speech of the same person represents a linguistic phenomenon of great historical significance. It indicates a population which was transferred or which emigrated of its free will from one dialectal area to another, where it acquired in time the dialect of that area, without forgetting its own.

---

[5](Editor's Note) We have recently become familiar with another aspect: the young people would deride those who had left the village and who, once they returned, spoke "differently", that is, they no longer spoke their native language. An apprentice shoemaker in Sagna (Nihai of Buium, who died on the battlefield in World War II), received the same treatment: when he finished his apprenticeship and came back dressed in German clothes, with a pocket-watch, and pronouncing correctly *zece* (ten). What's the time? Someone would ask when he showed up among the lads. "Ten ten" another would answer to the others' delight and despite the person who was the butt of their joke.

Chapter 16

A Description of the Dialect: Phonetics

Preliminary Considerations

The Romanian Chango dialect distinguishes itself through certain specific phonetical characteristics unknown to the Moldavian dialect. If the Changos had always lived in Moldavia, as Radu Rosetti considers,[1] today they would have to speak a pure Moldavian dialect.

There are three main characteristics that clearly differentiate the Chango dialect from the Moldavian dialect:

1) The affrication of the dental consonants /t/, /d/ followed by *e, i*. For example: *frunci* (for *frunti* = forehead), *munci* (for *munti* = mountain), *fraci* (for *frati* = brother), *ginci gi lapci* (for *dinti di lapti* = milk tooth).

2) The sibilant pronunciation /s/ : /ş/ and /z/ : /j/. For example: *sărpi* (pl. *sărki*) (for *şarpi* = snake), *săsî* (for *şăsî* = six), *cozoc* (for *cojoc* = sheepskin coat), *coazi* (for *coajî* = peel), *zaluzăli* (for *jaluzăli* = window blinds).

---

[1]Radu Rosetti, "Despre ungurii şi episcopatele catolice din Moldova" ("About the Hungarians and the Catholic Episcopates in Moldavia"), in *Analele Academiei Române. Memoriile secţiunii istorice,* seria II, vol. XXVII, 1904-1905, p. 248.

3) The preservation of /l'/ (palatal) not transformed into /i/, attested to by the verb "a lua" (to take): *eu l'eu, tu l'ei, el l'e, ei* (I take, you take, he takes, they take).

There are also some phonetical phenomena that the Chango dialect has in common with the Moldavian dialect: the palatalization of the labials /p/, /b/, /f/, /v/, /m/, the closing of the final vowels /ă/, /e/ to /î/, /i/ (*casî* for *casă* = house; *curcî* for *curcă* = turkey hen) and others, also present in the eastern Transylvanian dialects, with which we will not deal here.

The three phenomena we mentioned above, of which the first two are very frequent, confer this dialect with its characteristic affricative and sibilant Transylvanian individuality, more significant than the characteristics that differentiate, for instance, the Moldavian dialect from the Wallachian one.

Consequently, our observations will insist on the three phenomena, which represent the principal phonetical aspects inherited by the Chango dialect from its old Transylvanian dialectal base.

Let us discuss each of them separately.

1. The Affrication of the Dentals /t/, /d/ (+ *e, i*)

The Chango dialect does not know the dental occlusive /t/, /d/ followed by *e, i*, specific to the common Romanian language, or the dorsopalatals /t'/, /d'/ specific to Crişana and Maramureş,[2] but, as we have already shown, only /c/, /g/ affricated, like in some areas in Transylvania and the Banat: *minci* (for *minti* = mind), *saci* (for *sati* = villages), *bucaci* (for *bucati* = food), *feci* (for *feti* = girls), *carci* (for *carti* = book), *parci* (for *parti* = share), *părinci* (for *părinti* = parent), *micicel* (for *mititel* = little), *congei* (for *condei* = pen), *borgei* (for

---

[2]See Grigore Rusu, *op. cit.*

bordei = hovel), *dreptaci* (for *dreptati* = justice), *bunataci* (for *bunatati* = goodness), *space* (for *spati* = back), *gângesc* (for *gândesc* = I think), *sciu* (for *ştiu* = I know), *pucem* (for *putem* = we can), *Argal* (for *Ardeal* = Transylvania), *Cucuceni* (for *Cucuteni*).

The affricative pronunciation of the dentals /d/, /t/ gives the dialect a typically Transylvanian phonetical physiognomy. Here are a few texts with this pronunciation:[3]

> *Cuza n-o făcut dreptaci,*
> *Dumnedău sî-i facî parci.*
> *Gizaba ci scoli gi noapci,*
> *Dacî n-ai noroc nis parci...*
> *Druscili ca muscili*
> *Prăpăgesc găluscili...*
> *Trăsnascî-ci pucere*
> *a lui Dumnedău Sfântu!*

N-ai nis o *sococalî*-n capu tău, măi *băieci,* l'e sama, *sâlessci-ci* lanvăţăturî, fătu‚neu, cî *mincea-i pucerea* omului, nu coarnili, ca la *zici...* Vorba seluia:

> *Batî-ci pusciia minci,*
> *Cî n-ai fos măi ginăinci...*
> *Gin-i gi omu mincos*
> *Cî iel umblî cu folos.*

Cî *minci* ai *gistulî,* fărî *gicât* nu-i tătî bunî. Bagî-ţ în cap si-ţ spui, cî munca-i liacu sărăsiii, nu zoaca, nu *prosciia.* Sî măi ţăi *minci* una, cî *gin* boalî ci scoli, *gin* beţăii ci *tredăsc,* da *gin prosciii* niscacum. *Tredăsci* sî pun-*ci* pi *carci,* cî cu fotbalu sî cu ţâgara nimi nu s-o ferisit la igzamin. Sî dacî nu înţălez *gi* vorbî bunî, ieu oi sci sî grăiesc sî alfeli. Aud?...

---

[3]We are using the simplified phonetical transcription based on the *Atlasul linguistic român* (*The Romanian Linguistic Atlas*).

The affricative pronunciation of the consonants /t/, /d/ (+e, i) was also transmitted to the Hungarian Chango dialect. The bilingual inhabitants of Săbăoani pronounce in Hungarian *t + y, i* as *cs* (c): *kutya* (dog) is pronounced *kucso* (*cuco*), *mi atyánk* (our father) is pronounced *mi ocsánk* (*mi ocane*).

The Chango children learn in school to read and write and to recite poems according to literary Romanian phonetics. Outside the influence of school, under the influence of the family environment, they return to their traditional pronunciation.[4]

The presence of the phenomenon of affrication of the dentals in the Chango dialect reminds us of the similar phenomenon present in Transylvania and the Banat and justifies the conclusion that between

---

[4] I listened once to a child reciting a poem with the phonetics of the dialect he spoke at home:

Pi o stâncî niagrî, într-on veki *cascel,*

Ungi curzi-n vali on râu *micicel...*

On orolozu sunî *noapca zumataci,*

La *cascel* în poartî oari sâni *baci?*

"Very well, you recited the poem very well. But you must pronounce the words as you learned them in school: *castel, mititel.* And what is your name?"

"My name is *Scefănicî* Anton."

"Very well. now say it correctly, as you do at school: Şte-*fă-ni-că.*"

"I can't say it that way."

"Try and you will see that you can. Do you see this chocolate? If you say your name correctly..."

The boy stared at the tempting chocolate, changed his mind... The chocolate proved stronger than tradition. with an obvious exertion, as if he were taking medicine, he pronounced emphatically: *Şte-fă-ni-că* (Editor's Note: A similar observation can be made with regard to the children living in the villages about a hissing uttering from Oltenia. "The school struggles ineffectively against the altered pronunciation of /ş/ and /j/. Once they leave school, children utter /s/ and /z/ instead of /ş/ and /j/" (Mihail C. Gregorian, "Graiul din Oltenia nord-vestică şi Bănatul răsăritean" (II), in *Limba şi literature,* XXVI, 1970, p. 197).

this dialect and the dialects of certain Transylvanians there must have been a linguistic tie sometime in the past, a relation of origin, a connection of common living, and they must have had the same ethnic element, because such a characteristic and consistent phonetical concordance cannot be fortuitous. The fact that the Changos have been speaking for centuries with characteristics known only to Transylvanian dialects proves their Transylvanian Romanian origin. And the present phonetical dualism, confirming this conclusion, has a precise historical significance: before they had acquired the Moldavian dialect, they were speaking in their regional Transylvanian dialect.

When Radu Rosetti, in agreement with some Hungarian authors, maintained that the Changos had *always* lived in Moldavia, that is since the time of the founding of the principality or even before, he implicitly maintains a linguistic impossibility. It is impossible to conceive that, while living together with the Moldavians for supposedly six or seven centuries, the Changos would not have become accustomed to their dialect, but would have developed their own phonetical system, with sounds different from those they had been living with for such a long time, but at the same time identical with the sounds of some Romanian dialects from Transylvania and the Banat. If they were Hungarians who had *always* been living in Moldavia, they would have certainly been assimilated by the Moldavians long ago and today they would be speaking a perfect Moldavian dialect. To demonstrate this, let us analyze the case of the Changos of Szeckler origin living in the valley of the Trotuş River. These Szeckler refugees, who are improperly also called Changos, settled here following the bloody events at Madefalău in 1764. Over the course of two centuries, most of them acquired the Moldavian dialect so well that they cannot be differentiated from the Moldavians. How can we explain then the fact that the Romanian Changos on the valley of the Siret River, especially those in the northern group, speak with their family only in their own dialect, not in the Moldavian one? The answer is clear: because they were speaking this dialect when they were still in Transylvania, while the Szecklers we have referred to learned Romanian after they had settled in Moldavia. The error made by Radu Rosetti and by other historians is due to the fact that they thought that the inhabitants of the old Moldavian Catholic settlements from the thirteenth to the seventeenth centuries were Changos, but the Changos arrived here only in the eighteenth century.

2. The Sibilant Pronunciation (/s/ : /ş/ and /z/ : /j/)

The most characteristic phenomenon of the Chango dialect is the sibilant pronunciation (/s/ instead of /ş/ and /z/ instead of /j/), colloquially called *lisping* (Germ. *gelispelt*, Hung. *Sziszegō*). Talking about the same phenomenon in the Hungarian dialect of the Changos, Petru Zöld said: *quamquam hanc multo blesius efferent quam nos*,[5] they pronounce in a very lisping manner (Germ. *sehr unangenehm*).[6]

The Changos in Moldavia stigmatize and affricate any Romanian or foreign word they hear. The mill of *Schuller* (a German mechanic from long ago) was called *moara Suleriului* (= the mill of Suler) in the dialect of the population of Butea. An accountant, *Le Faucher*, of Swiss origin, was called *Lifosăriu*, and Dr. *Le Page*, a veterinarian of French origin, was *doftoru Lapăpazu.* The Italian missionary *Corradini* was called *părincili Coraginu.* Even the Latin hymn *Te Deum Laudamus* was pronounced *Ce Geum* by the old psalm reader Gârleanu, sometime in 1920-1921.[7] Today one can hear all the time

---

[5]Veszely, Imets *és* Kovács, *op. cit.,* p. 58.

[6]*Reise nach de Moldau*, p. 98.

[7]I once knew a few girls from the Catholic villages in the former county of Roman, who were attending courses at the Notre Dame de Sion Institute in Iaşi. In the first years of school, when they were not under the supervision of the nuns, these girls used

pronunciations like: *soferi* (for *şofer* = driver), *sancieri* (for *şantier* = construction site), *săginţi* (for *şedinţă* = meeting), *presăginci* (for *preşedinte* = president), *parcid* (for *partid* = party), *girecţâii* (for *direcţii* = directinos), *zurnal* (for *jurnal* = journal), *ambalaz* (for *ambalaj* = wrapping), *Cluz* (for *Cluj*), *Cecus* (for *Tecuci*), *Geva* (for *Deva*), *Cimisoara* (for *Timişoara*), etc.[8]

a. The Dating of the Phenomenon

Sigmatism is not attested to in any of the literary documents from the sixteenth century, an indication that this phenomenon was sporadic and preserved only in certain isolated localities, far from the great lines of communication. A series of old Romanian names with sibilant pronunciation were transmitted to the language of the Szecklers and have remained as such until today (*Kászon, Minisz, Kozán, Kozokár*).[9]

An isolated area, in which the population used this pronunciation, was the mountainous area in southeastern Transylvania (Ciuc, Giurgeu, Trei Scaune), the original native land of many Changos in

---

to pronounce the French language according to the sibilant tradition of the Romanian dialect they spoke at home: *saque zour* (for *chaque jour*), *zamais* (for *jamais*), *ze ne sais pas* (for *je ne sais pas*), *ze m'en vais au zardin* (for *je m'en vais au jardin*), a pronunciation that seemed easier and more natural to them than the French one. (Editor's Note: Elisabeta Ghercă, born in Iugani, a nun at Notre Dame of Sion in Paris, where she lived for a long time, speaks in a similar way: *saque zour, c'est a gire, zamasi de la vie,* to the listeners' amusement, who make fun at this *baragouin franco-roumain* (from D. Mărtinaş's notes).

[8](Editor's Note) "The driver Mihai Dămătar (from Butea, the author's note), who speaks correctly at work, but at home it comes easier to him to say: *somer, somează, viraz, rodaz, angazat, gepozit gi măcelărie, sancier, surub, masână, coleccivă, orăgim, girecţtie, săginţă, la* (in) *Cluz, la Cimişoara, la Ies*" (D. Mărtinaş, *Caietul* XVI, p. 231).

[9]See supra.

Moldavia.[10] The studies dealing with the history of the Romanian language do not mention the old sibilant regional pronunciation. Nevertheless, signs that indicate it are not lacking in documents, such as those pointed out in the studies of Mihail C. Gregorian[11] and Mircea Borcilă.[12]

The Changos used the sibilant pronunciation both in their Romanian dialect, as well as in the Hungarian dialect they adopted later, a fact noted by Petru Zöld in 1766.

Borrowing Zöld's term, the historian Engel confirms the sibilant pronunciation of the Changos: *nur redeten sie das ungarische blaese* (*schlirpend*), they speak Hungarian in a lisping manner.[13]

For the village Cleja (in the county of Bacău), the same pronunciation is attested to by Szarvas (1874)[14] and by Balaggi (1888).[15] At the beginning of the twentieth century, Rubinyi studied

---

[10]Veszley, Imets és Kovács, *op. cit.*, p. 61.

[11]Mihail C. Gregorian, *Graiul şi folclorul din Oltenia nord-vestică şi Bănatul răsăritean*, I, Craiova, 1938, p. 46.

[12]Originally from a village in the Banat with sibilant pronunciation, Mircea Borcilă dealt with this phonetical phenomenon in the following studies, without extending his area of research to Moldavia: "Un fenomen fonetic dialectal: rostirea lui /ş/ ca /s/ şi a lui /j/ ca /z/ în graiurile dacoromâne. I. Răspândirea şi situaţia actuală a fenomenului," in *Cercetări de lingvistică*, X, 1965, nr. 2, iulie-dec., pp. 269-279; "Un fenomen fonetic românesc dialectal: /ş/ : /s/ şi /j/ : /z/. II. Locul şi reflexele fenomenului în microsistemul graiului," *ibidem*, XI, 1966, nr. 1, ian.-iunie, pp. 71-76; "Un fenomen fonetic dialectal: rostirea lui /ş/ ca /s/ şi al lui /j/ ca /z/ în graiurile daco-române. Vechimea şi originea fenomenului," in *Studia Univeersitatis Babeş Bolyai*, seria Philologia, 1965, fasc. 2, pp. 109-119 (documentary attestations, pp. 115-116).

[13]Johann Christian Engel, *Gaschichte de Moldau und Walachey*, I, Halle 1804, p. 45.

[14]Szarvas Gábot, *op. cit.,* pp. 1-2.

[15]Les Hongrois en Moldavie, p. 215.

the sibilant pronunciation in a few villages in the county of Bacău and in Săbăoani (today in the county of Neamț).[16]

As we know, the sibilant pronunciation is not known to the Hungarian phonetical system. If this pronunciation is frequent in the small are of the Hungarian dialect in Moldavia, the explanation for this fact is that the speakers of this dialect are Szecklerized Romanians, and the sibilant phenomenon was transferred from Romanian into Hungarian, as a reflex of the adopted linguistic substratum.

In Moldavia this pronunciation was considered for a long time a corrupted, aberrant pronunciation, characteristic only of the Changos. The error is obvious, because the sibilant pronunciation represents a phenomenon characteristic of other regional dialects of the Romanian linguistic space as well, and in the past this phenomenon was much more widespread than today.

In the Banat, as we have already mentioned, this phonetical phenomenon was first pointed out by Enea Hodoş in 1892. He observed that in a few villages in the Banat, instead of the sound /ş/ people pronounced /s/.[17] The phenomenon is also pointed out by Gustav Weigand, in 1896, who also attests to the existence of the pronunciation of /z/ instead of /j/.[18] Regarding the range of the phenomenon (the German linguist had recorded it in only four villages). Hodoş specifies in another collection of popular poems: "In the Banat there are… five villages where the sounds /ş/, /j/ are replaced by /s/, /z/, namely: Ilova, Poiana, Țerova, Visag, and Cuptoare. And if in some of these villages the old pronunciation is slowly disappearing… I can say with a great degree of certainty that in some villages in the neighboring areas this habit disappeared before

---

[16]Rubinyi Mózes, *op. cit.*, pp. 62-63.

[17]Enea Hodoş, *Poesii poporale* din *Banat*, p. 5.

[18]Gustav Weigand, *Der banater Dialekt*, Leipzig, 1896, pp. 32-34.

anyone thought of undertaking the necessary investigations to study these Romanian subdialects.[19]

This pronunciation was attested in the village Cuptoare, also in a Banat glossary from 1886, published by Pia Gradea. Here people pronounced: *cas* (for *caş*), *sură* (for *şură*), *besică* (for *beşică*), *săd* (for *şăd*), *săzătoare* (for *şăzătoare*), *zudecată* (for *judecată*), etc.[20]

The existence of the stigmatism in Visag as well, contested by Weigand and maintained by Hodoş, is confirmed by the answer to Hasdeu's questionnaire, sent by the local schoolteacher Liviu Iancu, on 13/1 March 1885, in which it is specified that "instead of /ş/, one can very often hear /s/, for example: *asa* for *aşa*, *si* for *şi*, *septe* for *şepte*, *sasă* for *şasă*."[21]

In 1900, Weigand noticed this phenomenon also in western Oltenia, in the localities of Siroca, Balta, Malarişca, Gorneşti, Presna, Costeşti, Gornoviţa, Cenavârf, Nadanova, Izverna, Seliştea, Obârşia, Merişeşti, Orieşti,[22] Sohodol, and Cloşani, observing the fact that here /z/ never appeared.[23] The sibilant phenomenon in Oltenia was later on also studied by Mihail C. Gregorian, who noted that this pronunciation was still generalized in the villages in the mountainous region of the county of Mehedinţi: Gormenţi (with Camăna), Costeşti, Prejna, Gornoviţa, and Obârşia-Cloşani. From here it extended to the south (Podeni, especially the hamlet Malovanul), to the east (Malarişca,

---

[19]Enea, Hodoş, *Cântece bănăţene*. With an answer to Gustav Weigand, Caransebeş, 1898, p. 11.

[20]Pia Gradea, "O culegere de cuvinte bănăţene," in *Materiale şi cercetări dialectale*, I, 1960, p. 131.

[21]*Ibidem*, note 32.

[22](Editor's Note) The locality of Orieşti does not exist, having been mistakenly registered, instead of Orzeşti, mentioned by Gregorian.

[23]Gustav Weigand, "Die rumanische Dialekte des Kleinen Walachei...," in *Siebenter Jachresbericht...*, 1900, p. 50.

Sfodia, and Balta, sporadically), to the north (Nadanova, Canicea, and Izverna), and to the northeast (Ponoare, Gărdăneasa, Băluţa, and Ludu, with reduced influence). Sporadically, it is also present in Cloşani and Orzeşti.[24]

The last scholarly researcher of the sibilant pronunciation in Oltenia is Valeriu Rusu, in a study about the consonant /ş/.[25]

A remainder of this pronunciation can be noticed in Nadăşu (in the county of Cluj), where the pronunciation *cirese*, instead of *cireşe* (cherries) is preserved, a term used for a sewing patter on the women's *chimeşi* (shirts).[26]

According to oral information, which we could not verify, the phenomenon is sporadically present in other regions of Transylvania as well.

We will not discuss the existence of the phenomenon in the Istro-Romanian dialect and in the dialect of some Macedo-Romanians in northern Greece, where it is probably the result of foreign adstrata, which does not, however, exclude the possibility of its belonging to the proto-Romanian substratum.

If in our study of the Changos we have stressed too much the existence of the phenomenon of sibilant pronunciation in other

---

[24]Mihail C. Gregorian, *op. cit.*, pp. 44-45 (Editor's Note: See Mihail C. Gregorian, *op. cit.*, pp. 197-198; idem, *Folelor din Oltenia şi Muntenia*, I, Bucureşti, 1967, passim (sibilant texts).

[25]Valeriu Rusu, "Consoana /ş/ în limba română," in *Studii şi cercetări linguistice*, XVIII, 1967, nr. 2, pp. 181-183 (Editor's Note: See idem, *Graiul din nord-vestul Olteniei*, Bucureşti, 1971, pp. 94-96. See also Radu Sp. Poescu, *Graiul gorjenilor de lîngă munte*, Craiova, 1980, pp. 52-53, where this phenomenon is called *zetacism*).

[26]G/T/ Niculescu-Varone, *Costumele naţionale din România întregită*, Bucureşti, 1937, p. 81. (Editor's Note: The phonetism *cireasă*, cirese is very frequent in Transylvania even in its proper sense (see *NALR pe* regiuni. Transilvania, chestiunea 1169; manuscript belonging the Institute of Linguistics in Cluj-Napoca).

regional dialects as well, we have done so with the purpose of demonstrating that this pronunciation is not aberrant and is not due to some strangers who speak Romanian in a degraded manner, but, on the contrary, it is an old phonetical phenomenon, present not only in the dialect of the Changos, but in other regions of the Dacian-Romanian linguistic territory as well, a phenomenon whose origins go far back in the past, both in the Romanian language as well as in other European countries, as far back as the period of the formation of the respective languages and peoples.

The presence of this phonetical phenomenon in the old dialect of the Changos does not prove the foreign origin of its speakers, but, on the contrary, it illustrates their Romanian belonging; throughout history they have preserved an archaic phenomenon that disappeared from the contemporary language, and, due to special historical circumstances, was best preserved in this Transylvanian dialect.

This phenomenon is perceived everywhere as old-fashioned and outdated, explaining why it is now in a regressive phase, close to almost completely disappearing. A vestige from the historical development of the Romanian language, it is still maintained today in two areas where the Dacian-Romanian language evolved: sporadically on the verge of disappearance, in the Banat and northwestern Oltenia; still strong, but at the same time in regression, in Moldavia, being present in the dialect of the approximately 180,000 speakers of Romanian in the 170 villages with a Catholic population in the counties of Bacău, Neamţ, and Iaşi. Seen from the perspective of the evolution of the language, after a few generations the phenomenon is destined to total disappearance.

b. The pronunciation /s/ : /ş/

The phonetical tradition of the Chango dialect never tolerates the whistling consonant /ş/, which is always pronounced /s/, in any conditions and in any position. It receives only one treatment: *sărpi, săsî, săpci, chimesî, rusâni, senusî, mătusî, lesâii, usî, cas, closci, puisor, cucos, bors, căus, sâpot, pocris, bătăus, sâres, oras, sârag, mos, moasî, a prăsî, a gresî, a isî, Tămăsan, Fărcăsan, Niclăusan, Ies, Petrisor, Scheia, Cimisăsci, Habăsăsci, Focsăn.* The reason for this ancestral intolerance is hard to specify, it is probably a tendency inherited from the substratum.

The sibilant consonant /s/, as well as other consonants, having a hard character, conditions very strongly the vowels /i/, /e/ which follow it, changing them into /î/ and /ă/. Thus: /i/ preceded by /s/ > /î/ (*sî, sâret, sânî, a păsî, a sfârsî*); /e/ final preceded by /s/ > /ă/ > /î/ (*flori frumoasî, vaci grasî*); the reflexive pronoun *se* and the conjunction *sî* are pronounced /sî/ (*sî sî ducî sî sî speli; sî chei gin faţa me, sî nu ci văd*).

The sibilant pronunciation and the always hard character of the consonant *s* gave birth to an interesting morphologic phenomenon: the homonymy of the singular with the plural of the nouns and the adjectives with the theme in /s/ (or, in other words, the neutralization of the singular-plural opposition). Thus:

singular: un om **frumos**	plural: doi oamini **frumos**
	(instead of **frumoşi**)
(a handsome man)	(two handsome men)
un om **sănătos**	doi oamini **sănătos**
	(instead of **sănătoşi**)
(a healthy man)	(two healthy men)

un **urs** bătrân	doi **urs** bătrâni (instead of **urşi**)
(an old bear)	(two old bears)
un **ţărus** lung	doi **ţărus** lungi (instead of **ţăruşi**)
(a long stake)	(two long stakes)
un chipărus gras	doi chipărus gras
	(instead of chipăruşi graşi)
(a green pepper)	(two green peppers)

In only one case, the same phenomenon appears identically in the dialect of the Istro-Romanians in Suşnieviţa,[27] although no territorial connection has ever existed between the two dialects, and their historical evolution took place in different conditions.

c. The pronunciation /z/ : /j/

The same phonetical tradition does not tolerate the whistling consonant /j/, which in the old Slavic words is always pronounced /z/. For example: *cozoc* (for *cojoc* = sheepskin coat), *coazî* (for *coajî* = peel), *grizî* (for *grijî* = worry), *tânjalî* = double carriage-pole), *Bezan* (for *Bejan*), *Cozan* (for *Cojan*), *Burduzăni* (for *Burdujăni*).

Mention should be made that, while the whistling consonant knows only one treatment, the whistling consonant /j/ of the common Romanian language knows two treatments:

a) in words of Slavic origin and in the neologisms that have recently entered the dialect, /j/ is pronounced /z/ : *strazî* (for *strajî* = guard), *cârzî* (for *cârjî* = walking stick), *pârzol* (for *pârjol* = fire), *zaracic* (for *jăratec* = embers), *rogozânî* (for *rogojinî* = mat), *vlăzgan* (for *vlăjgan* = stalwart fellow), *a prăzî* (for *a prăjî* = to fry), *a grizî* (for *a grijî* = to take care of), *a sluzî* (for *a slujî* = to serve), *bagaz* (for

---

[27]Sextil Puşcariu, *Studii istro-române*, II, Bucureşti, 1926, p. 121.

bagaj = luggage), *grilaz* (for *grilaj* = railing), *rodaz* (for *rodaj* = running in), *pontaz* (for *pontaj* = clocking), *zambon* (for *jambon* = ham), *angazament* (for *angajament* = commitment).

b) in the words of Latin origin, /j/ of the literary language is always pronounced as constrictive /z/ : *zoc* (for *joc* = game), *zos* (for *jos* = down), *zug* (for *jug* = yoke), *azung* (for *ajung* = I arrive), *zumataci* (for *jumătate* = half), *împrezur* (for *împrejur* = around), *zuncan* (for *juncan* = young bull), *zugeţ* (for *judeţ* = trail), *zugicatî* (for *judecată* = judgement).

The difference is obvious in the following saying: *zocu sparzi cozocu* (*zoc* < Lat. *iocus; cozoc* < old Slav. *kozuhu*).

The rule applies consistently, with no exception. In the common language, words of Latin origin are perfectly differentiated from those of Slavic origin. A Latin word is never pronounced with /z/ and a Slavic word is never pronounced with /s/.

What is the explanation? We believe the following considerations can provide the answer:

The whistling consonant /j/ of Slavic origin entered the Romanian language, with Slavic words, sometime around the seventh to the ninth centuries, and it remained as such until today. In the sibilant dialects, in which the speakers did not tolerate the whistling consonant /ş/, they could neither tolerate the whistling consonant /j/, which they interpreted as /z/ (*cozoc, coazî,* instead of *cojoc, coajă*), and this is how it has been preserved until today.

The evolution of the Latin *yod* was different. According to the norms of the historical phonology of the Romanian language, the Latin *yod* went through the following phonetical phases: /i/ > /g/ > /j/, as in the series:

iocum > goc > joc (game)
iovem > goi > joi (Thursday)

iuri > gur > jur (I swear)[28]

When the Slavic words entered the Romanian language, the Latin *yod* had reached the phase /g/ (*goc, goi, gur*). It continued its evolution going successively through the phase /z/ (*z*), and in the eighteenth century it reached, in part of the Dacian-Romanian linguistic territory, the present phase /j/ (*joc, joi, jur*).

The sibilant dialect of the Changos, which did not tolerate the whistling consonant /j/, stopped at the previous phase /z/, like in Moldavia, a great part of Transylvania, and the Banat, and it has remained as such until today.

From all this we can draw the following conclusions:

1. The sibilant dialect went through the same evolutionary phonetical process, from the Latin *yod* to the phase /z/, as other Dacian-Romanian dialects. In other words, the ancestors of the Changos spoke Romanian *ab initio*, from the period of the formation of the Romanian language and the Romanian people.

2. If the Changos were Romanianized Hungarians and recently assimilated by the Romanians, they would have to speak the Moldavian dialect. In reality, the double treatment of the consonant /j/ as /z/ and /z/, and not /j/ (as in the Moldavian dialect), clearly differentiates the two dialects.

3. The fact that the Slavic /j/ was received as /z/ in the sibilant dialects is not just a supposition, as it is still occurring today. Any kind of /j/, regardless of its origin, that enters the Chango dialect toady, is automatically received as /z/: *zurnal* (instead of *jurnal*), *angazament* (instead of *angajament*), and even *bonzur* (instead of *bonjur* < Fr. *bon*

---

[28]See Al. Rosetti, *Istoria limbii române*, IV, V, VI, Bucureşti, 1966, p. 54; I. Şiadbei, "Contribuţii la studiul latinei orientale," in *Studii şi cercetări linguistice*, III, 1957, nr. 4, p. 486; Floraica Dumitrescu, *Introducere în fonetica istorică a limbii române*, Bucureşti, 1967, p. 109.

jour). It is obvious that in these cases we are not dealing with regressive process from /j/ to /z/, due to an internal process of development of the language, but with a spontaneous transformation of /j/ as /z/, probably because of an intolerance due to the substratum.

* * *

According to Weigand, the sibilant pronunciation raises two related problems: the origin of this phenomenon and the origin of its speakers.

Consequently, by approaching the problem of the phenomenon we will approach, *eo ipso,* also the problem of the origin of the Changos.

Regarding the origin of this phenomenon in the Romanian language spoken by the Changos, two controversial hypothesis circulated in the past: one supposing a Cuman origin and the other a Hungarian origin.

d. The Hypothesis of the Cuman Origin of the Phenomenon

Romanian scholars did not pay any attention to the sibilant pronunciation of the Romanian Chango dialect, or, if they briefly pointed it out, they had the tendency to see it as the degraded pronunciation of speakers of foreign origin.

The Hungarian researchers of the Hungarian Chango dialect studied it with much interest. There was a time when all the enigmatic aspects of the problem of the Changos were attributed to a presumed Cuman influence. Weigand saw in the Changos of sibilant dialect the remnant of Magyarized Cumans, who had recently been Romanianized by the Moldavians, and in the sibilant pronunciation he saw a heritage from the old language of their Cuman ancestors. He did not produce, however, convincing evidence to support his hypothesis. Generally, the German linguist treated this problem too hastily. He did not even consider the question: if the Changos were Romanianized by the Moldavians, why is it that they do not speak their dialect? The Hungarian linguist Melich János proved with arguments considered unanimously valid that the sibilant pronunciation of the Hungarian Chango dialect has nothing in common with the Cuman language.[29] The present descendants of the Cumans, whom we know for certain settled in the thirteenth century between the Tisa and the Danube rivers, today assimilated by the Hungarians, did not preserve in their present Hungarian language any trace of sibilant pronunciation. As a result, Hungarian linguists abandoned the hypothesis of the Cuman origin of this phenomenon, considering it obsolete.[30] Therefore, the origin of this phenomenon, both in the Romanian as well as in the Hungarian Chango dialect will have to be sought elsewhere.

e. The Hypothesis of the Hungarian Origin of the Phenomenon

Other authors presumed, but without plausible arguments, that the phenomenon would be a remnant of the dialect of the Hungarians from Atelkuz, and the Changos would be the descendants of some Atelkuzian Hungarians established in Moldavia in the tenth century.[31] The difficult part of the problem is that the language of those

---

[29]Melich János, *op. cit.,* (Editor's Note: See a bibliography of the research on the Phonetics and Morphology of Language in *Codex Cumanicus* (1942-1962), by Vladimir Drîmba, *Syntaxe comane,* Bucureşti-Leiden, 1973, p. 3, note 1; texts from *Codex Comanicus,* ibidem, pp. 189-329. A list of words taken from this text can be found in *Originea românilor by* Alexandru Phillipide, II, Iaşi, 1928, pp. 354-357).

[30]Mikecs Lászlo, *op. cit.,* p. 43.

[31]Györffy István, *op. cit.,* pp. 68-74.

Hungarians is not known to us. We do not know whether it had this phonetical phenomenon or not. And, if the Changos are Atelkuzian Hungarians who settled in Moldavia, how did they come to speak Romanian with a Transylvanian dialect?

According to the hypothesis of Gábor Lnkö, the phenomenon would have been inherited in the Hungarian Chango dialect from the dialect of a Hungarian population that would have lived in the eleventh and twelfth centuries in the regions of the Tisa and Someş rivers, a dialect in which /ş/, /j/, and /c/ were replaced by /s/, /z/, and /ţ/.[32] Unfortunately, the dialect of this presumed population did not leave any documentary traces and is completely unknown, thus this hypothesis would need more solid evidence to receive serious consideration by scholars.

More recently, Géza Báko formulated the hypothesis that the sibilant pronunciation of the Changos would be a reflex of a Pannonian-Slavic influence, from the time when their distant ancestors lived in the Raba region, on the western frontier of Hungary (from the eleventh to the thirteenth centuries). In the thirteenth century these Hungarians were transferred for military purposes to the eastern part of the Hungarian kingdom (southeastern Transylvania), from where, in time, they crossed into Moldavia.[33] According to this hypothesis, the descendants of these western Hungarians would be the present-day Changos. The first problem with this hypothesis is that it cannot be established whether the sibilant pronunciation of the dialect of the Hungarians in Raba represents a Pannonian-Slavic influence,

---

[32]Lnkö Gábor, *A moldvai csángók. I. A csángók kapcsolatai az erdélyi magyarsággal* (*The Changos in Moldavia. I. The Connections of the Changos with the Hungarians in Transylvania*), Budapest, 1936, p. 26.

[33]Bakó Géza, *op. cit.*, pp. 39-41.

as the author presumes, or a Roman-Pannonian influence. Because this is what Anonymous wrote about the Romans in Pannonia, called *pastores romanorum,* meaning the Romanian Wallachians: *Et inde egressi usque ad Rabam er Rebuceam venerunt. Sclavorum et Pannoniorum gentes et regna vastaverunt er eorum regions occupaverant... et Romanos fugatos esse de Pannonia per ipsos* ("And leaving here, they arrived at Raba and Rebucea. [The Hungarians] pillaged the countries and the people of the Slavs and the Pannonians and occupied their lands... and the Romans were driven away from Pannonia by them").[34]

It results, first of all, that the ones who transmitted the sibilant pronunciation to the dialect of the Hungarians in Raba were Pannonian Romanians (*pastores romanorum,* the Wallachians), driven away from Pannonia by the Hungarians to this region, where they were in time assimilated by them. Therefore, a Roman-Pannonian influence is more probable, namely Romanian, rather than a Slavic-Pannonian one, as the author argues.

Secondly, there is no documentary evidence which indicates that the Hungarians in Raba moved all the way to southeastern Transylvania. There is no basis for this hypothesis.

Third, for explaining the origin of the sibilant pronunciation in the Hungarian dialect of the Changos in Moldavia there is no need to resort to the dialect of the Hungarians in Raba, with whom it is certain that the Romanian ancestors of the bilingual Changos had no connection whatsoever. It is sufficient to know that this pronunciation is the most characteristic phenomenon of the Romanian dialect of the

---

[34]N. Drăganu, *op. cit.,* pp. 542-543 (Editor's Note: See the same next in *Izvoarele istoriei românilor* by G. Popa-Lisseanu I, Bucureşti, 1934, pp. 62-63).

Szecklerized Romanians. In the process of Szecklerization, their traditional sibilant pronunciation was transferred from their old Romanian dialect to the adopted Hungarian dialect, as a reflex of the Romanian stratum over the Szeckler superstratum. This renders implausible the hypothesis of a Pannonian-Slavic influence or of a Hungarian influence from the regions of the Tisa and the Someş on the Hungarian Chango dialect. During the period of Szecklerization, the predecessors of the Changos did not need any foreign influence from which to receive their sibilant pronunciation, which they already knew very well from their own Romanian dialect.

From the hypothesis of Géza Bakó we can, however, keep in mind the detail that, in regional Hungarian dialects, whenever, accidentally and transitorily, the phenomenon of the pronunciation /sz/ : /s/ (Rom. /ş/ : /s/) is encouraged (for example in the Raba region), it is due to a foreign, non-Magyar influence. Being foreign and therefore inviable, this pronunciation disappeared in time, because it was not a native phenomenon. Only the Hungarian dialect of the Changos in Moldavia is an exception to this rule, because they are Szecklerized Romanians. While the linguistic consciousness manifests aversion and phonetical incompatibility toward the sibilant pronunciation, perceiving it as a corrupted pronunciation, alien to the spirit of the Hungarian language, the Changos, on the contrary, use this pronunciation consistently, both in Romanian as well as in Hungarian, and do not renounce it easily the cause of this propensity toward the pronunciation with /s/ lies in the fact that with them the phenomenon is ancient. Like other phenomena, the sibilant pronunciation, so tenacious in the Hungarian dialect of some Changos, represents linguistic proof of their Romanian origin. In the process of their linguistic assimilation by the Szecklers, the Changos adopted the material elements of the Hungarian language, the lexicology and the grammar, but they could not acquire the Finno-Ugric phonetical system of this language, which they replaced with the pronunciation of their original dialect, shaping the Hungarian linguistic material in the phonetical mold of their basic Romanian dialect. In the localities in which they experienced a long-standing Szeckler influence, as happened in the villages in the Szeckler region, the sibilant pronunciation disappeared in time, although sporadic traces of the phenomenon still exist here and there, as Géza Bakó informs us. After the emigration of the Changos to Moldavia, the unifying influence of the Hungarian language having ceased, especially in the villages in the northern group (for example in Săbăoani), this pronunciation was preserved unaltered, because it found support in the Romanian linguistic stratum of the speakers.

f. The Proto-Romanian (Latin) Origin

Some observers saw in the sibilant pronunciation of the Changos a linguistic anomaly, due to the inability of some foreigners to adjust themselves to the Romanian phonetical system. The facts do not support this thesis. The Romanian Chango dialect went through the same stages of development as other Transylvanian dialects. The same sibilant pronunciation in the dialect of some speakers from the Banat and Oltenia was never considered aberrant, a phonetical anomaly, a conclusion which is also valid for the dialect of the Changos. They pronounce correctly the Romanian characteristic sounds, difficult to pronounce for non-Romanians, like the vowels /ă/, /î/, the fricatives /s/, /z/, the diphthongs *ea, oa, au, îi,* and when they use the Moldavian dialect they pronounce normally the whistling consonants /ş/, /j/ which their phonetical tradition does not tolerate in their own dialect.

Mircea Borcilă believes that there is no connection between the phenomenon of the pronunciation /s/ : /ş/ in the Banat and the same phenomenon in Moldavia.[1] On the contrary, Weigand considers that, naturally, the isolated appearance of this linguistic phenomenon in Moldavia, Oltenia, and the Banat is out of the question, that it must be based on a "common ethnographic element."[2]

The opinion of the German linguist in this regard appears perfectly logical, because, as we are trying to demonstrate, this pronunciation represents the same phenomenon in all Dacian-Romanian dialects, due to a common origin and causes. Besides the sibilant pronunciation, the Chango dialect has another phonetical phenomenon in common with the dialect of the Banat: the affrication of the dentals /t/, /d/ followed by *e, i.* The Changos pronounce like the people from the Banat: *frunce* (for *frunte* = forehead), *mince* (for *minte* = mind), *lapce* (for *lapte* = milk), *vesced* (for *veşted* = withered).[3] Could this be a simple coincidence, or is it due to a common historical phonetical evolution in the distant past? Less inspired was Weigand's opinion when he maintained that the people of sibilant dialect in the Banat would be Romanianized Changos, losing sight of the fact that, when the first colonies of Changos were brought to the Banat,[4] the people there had been using this pronunciation for centuries. Therefore they could not have acquired it from the Changos.

Dismissing for valid reasons the hypothesis of the Cuman or Magyar origin of the phenomenon, Mircea Borcilă considers that the pronunciation /s/ : /ş/ is a Romanian phonetical phenomenon, the result

---

[1] Mircea Borcilă, "Un fenomen fonetic dialectal...," in *Studia...*, p. 110.

[2] Gustav Weigand, *Der Ursprung der s-Gemeinden*, p. 137.

[3] We will not take into account the softer character of these secondary affricate consonants in the Banat than in the Transylvanian dialects in which they still exist and than in the dialect of the Changos in Moldavia, as it is the same process of affrication of the dentals.

[4] (Editor's Note) The Changos were colonized in the Banat, beginning in 1880.

of an internal process in the development of the Romanian language.[5] This would be a process of depalatalization of /ş/, which, he believes, could be part of a more general tendency, which appears in the Romanian language as a consequence of Slavic influence.[6] This is very unlikely. What seemed to Mircea Borcilă to be examples of depalatalization of /ş/ attested to in the fourteenth and fifteenth centuries (the toponyms *Vizak, Visak,* instead of *Vişag,* and *Russova, Riszova,* instead of *Ruşova*) is in fact the sibilant pronunciation of these toponyms.

This hypothesis raises some doubts. The internal process of development of the Romanian language always went in the direction of the palatalization of the Latin primitive /s/ followed by /i/, and it cannot be demonstrated that this process would have been inverted later on, going from /ş/ to /s/, due to an obscure cause.

It is unlikely that the pronunciation /s/ : /ş/ would be the result of a phonetical regression (/ş/ > /s/) or even a phenomenon borrowed from the Slavs, when – and this is certain – the pronunciation with the primitive, unpalatalized /s/ was characteristic of vulgar Latin and afterwards of proto-Romanian from the fifth to the seventh centuries. This is the objective linguistic fact which preceded and, logically, was at the basis of the sibilant pronunciation. With the existence of indisputable linguistic proof in the primitive Romanian language itself, no doubtful speculations regarding an uncertain Pannonian-Slavic origin of this phenomenon are necessary, the more so as it is also present in the Western Romance idioms as well, in which any hypothesis of a Slavic origin is excluded. Weigand noted the pronunciation of /s/ among the Macedo-Romanians in the region of Olympus, for example *arsune* (for *ruşine* = shame), *aros* (for *roş* =

---

[5]Mircea Borcilă, *op. cit.,* p. 118.

[6]*Ibidem,* p. 117.

red), and so on, his opinion being that the phenomenon was due to Greek influence.[7] This is possible, but not certain, because the phenomenon, as we have seen, is found also in certain Daco-Romanian regional dialects (people in the Banat and the Changos pronounce *rusâne* and *ros*) where the possibility of Greek influence is excluded.

Emil Petrovici considers that the pronunciation /s/ : /ş/ represents a phenomenon of phonological subdifferentiation or of the losing of the whistling consonants by their fusion with sibilant consonants, due to the influence of either the substratum or of the adstratum.[8] Without giving a categorical verdict regarding the origin of the phenomenon, Petrovici does not exclude the possibility of a phonetical inheritance from the substratum, and in this case it cannot be a question of phonological subdifferentiation or of the losing the whistling consonants, but of the preservation of the primitive sibilants of the Latin substratum.

Valeriu Rusu, who studied the phenomenon in the dialect spoken in northwestern Oltenia, considers that it could be the result of a local process of rearrangement of the consonantal system, due to the reaction of the speakers against the identification of /s/ and /ş/, and of the realization of new relations in the system of the consonants /ş/ - /s/ and /s/ - /s/.[9] Thus, a complicated, doubtful solution is preferred to a clear and logical one that integrates the sibilant pronunciation perfectly in the Latin substratum of the Romanian language.

---

[7]Gustav Weigand, *Die Sprache der Olympo-Walachen*, Leipzig, 1888, pp. 52-53; see also Th. Capidan, *Aromânii. Dialectul aromân*, Bucureşti, 1932, pp. 334-335.

[8]Emil Petrovici, "Interpénétration des systèmes linguistiques," in *Actes du X-e Congrès International des Linguistes...*, I, Bucarest, 1969, p. 43 (Editor's Note: See also the Romanian version "Întrepătrunderea sistemelor linguistice," in *Studii de slavistică*, I, 1969, p. 75).

[9]Valeriu Rusu, *op. cit.*, p. 182.

All these three hypotheses see in the sibilant pronunciation a Romanian phonetical phenomenon or, at least, one that appeared on Romanian territory. Without denying it, they avoid, however, the hypothesis of the preservation of a proto-Romanian pronunciation, inherited from vulgar Latin. Is there enough evidence supporting such a hypothesis?

Any careful observer would be struck by the phonetical correspondence between the vulgar Latin pronunciation with /s/ + /i/ unpalatalized and the identical pronunciation of the Daco-Romanian sibilant dialects; for example: Lat. *tussire* as compared to the present *tusâre* (cough), *serpem* as compared to *sarpe* and *sărpe* (snake), *sesse* as compared to *sase* and *săse* (six), *insellare* as compared to *înselare* (deceit), *sessum* as compared to *săs* (plain), *caseum* as compared to *cas* (pot cheese), etc.

The same ties can also be noted between the Latin pronunciation and some western Romance dialects:

Lat. *tussire* as compared to old Fr. *toussir,* It. *tossir,* Eng. *tussir;*

Serpem	It., Port. serpe, Sp. sierpe, Eng. serp;
lixivia	Piem, lessie, Mil. Lesia, Fr. lessive, Rom. lesâie;
sesse	Eng. ses, Sp., Port. seis, Fr. six, Frl. sis;
sessum	It., Port., sesse, Sp. siese, old Fr. ses;
caseum	Sard. casu.

If the Western Romance phonetical correspondences represent, without any doubt, a direct filiation, a continuation of vulgar Latin phonetical sounds, the question is: is the same conclusion valid in the cases of the Daco-Romanian sibilant dialects as well? This is a hypothesis that cannot be excluded. The more so as the comparison with other Romance idioms is a sure method for establishing the Romance character (Latin origin) of certain linguistic phenomena.

Indeed, if the Sarinian *casu* is, without any doubt, the Latin reflex *casseus,* through direct filiation, could we actually maintain that the Daco-Romanian sibilant form *casu* is the result of a phonetical regression *caş>cas,* or even the result of Slavic influence? Such a supposition cannot be accepted.

Let us examine this phenomenon in other European languages and dialects.

In the Polish language the dialectal sibilant pronunciation, called *mazurzenie,* is the most characteristic phonetical feature of the dialect of the Mazurs, who live in Mazovia and Malopolska. Polish Slavicists, among them the erudite dialectologist Kazimierz Nitsch,[10] agree that this is a phonetical phenomenon of archaic origin, inherited from proto-Slavonic, due to a Baltic substratum, the dialect of the Iatvings. The phenomenon disappeared from the common Polish language, but has been preserved in the dialect of the Mazurs. Let us keep this in mind: the phenomenon is inherited from proto-Slavonic.[11]

In the German dialect *plattdeutsch,* in contrast with literary German, the consonantal /st/, /sp/ are pronounced with pure, unpalatalized /s/ : for example *sterben* (to die) and *Spiel* (game), in which the consonantal groups /st/, /sp/ are heard like in the Romanian words *mister* (mystery), *spirală* (spiral). German philologists agree that this phenomenon represents the preservation of an archaic proto-German pronunciation, inherited from Indo-European. This pronunciation has been preserved, dialectically, also in the northern Germanic languages. It has been established that in all these languages the phenomenon is inherited from the common proto-German.

It is well-known that the pronunciation with primitive /s/ was also preserved in Greek and Latin.

---

[10]Kazimierz Nitsch, *Wybór pism polonistycznuch*, I, Wroclaw, 1954, p. 195.

[11]This phenomenon is also known in Russian under the name of *cokanje.*

The preservation of this pronunciation in so many different languages, dialects, and territories, by so many different peoples, implies an ancient common linguistic base. It is a matter of preservation of a primitive stage of pronunciation, through numerous ethno-linguistic stratifications, generated by the perpetual succession of historical events. It is an ancient phenomenon, inherited – according to the common opinion of the linguists – from the proto-Slavonic, and respectively proto-German substratums, which, in their turn, inherited it from the common Indo-European substratum.

With regard to the same pronunciation in some Daco-Romanian dialects, the logical hypothesis is that the same phenomenon in these dialects must have the same very old origin as in other European languages and dialects. Consequently, it represents a phonetical inheritance from the primitive Romanian, which, in its turn, inherited it directly from the vulgar Latin language, and the latter from Indo-European.

General linguistics teaches us that any phonetical transformation of great proportions, as was the palatalization of the Latin /s/ followed by /i/, which appeared in the fifth and sixth centuries, does not happen suddenly, but develops slowly, and is generalized progressively. At the end of the first millennium, the pronunciation with /s/ had not yet disappeared from all Daco-Romanian dialects. It was still present in southeastern Transylvania in the fourteenth century.[12]

The fact that this phenomenon has been maintained up to the present-day in some southwestern Daco-Romanian dialects supports the thesis that it was also preserved in the Romanian-Pannonian dialects of the first millennium, which, before the coming of the Hungarians, had lived and developed in close vicinity and in direct contact with these dialects.

---

[12]See *supra,* p. 62.

It was this old southwestern dialectal area from which the sibilant dialect of the Romanians in southeastern Transylvania resulted, who, following the process of Szecklerization, will receive from the Szecklers the name of Changos. In summary, the linguistic considerations that determine us to see in the sibilant pronunciation an archaic remnant, inherited from Latin and proto-Romanian, are the following:

1. The pronunciation with primitive Indo-European /s/, transmitted to the main languages in Europe, like old German, Slavonic, Greek, and Latin, constituted ever since the archaic period, a norm for the Indo-European peoples in Europe, including the Romans. This kind of pronunciation could not suddenly disappear from the primitive Romanian of the fifth and sixth centuries, when the palatalization of /s/ + /i/ made its appearance. It continued its existence for centuries in isolated areas (in some southwestern dialects and in the dialect of southeastern Transylvania).

2. If, over a long period of time, a phenomenon is attested again and again in the same place, with no evidence of an outside origin for it, it must be admitted that it continued incessantly on the respective territory. The phenomenon of sibilant pronunciation is still preserved in some dialects in the Banat and Oltenia, and it is not possible to prove a different origin of it, after it was attested to in the primitive Romanian language. Consequently, one must admit that it continued incessantly since that time on this territory.

3. The historical phonetics of the Romanian language did not and still does not know any internal cause so strong and efficient to be able to eliminate a phonetical tradition of such proportions as the palatalization of /s/ followed by /i/, which appeared in the fifth and sixth centuries and was later generalized in the Romanian language. If such a cause had existed as the result of an internal process of development of the language, it would have also affected other dialects

of the Romanian language, it would have also affected other dialects of the Romanian language, which did not happen. In the phonetical evolution of the Romanian language there are other archaic phenomena as well, preserved at a local level, after they had evolved in the other Dacian-Romanian dialects. An example of this is the preservation of the proto-Romanian /n/ (for instance *vine* < Lat. *vinea* for *vie* [vineyard], *cun* < Lat. *cuneus* for *cui* [nail]) in the Banat. Just as the people from the Banat pronounce today *vinye* and *cuny* cu /ny/ from proto-Romanian, they also pronounce *sase* and *sarpe* (for *şase* = six and *şarpe* = snake) with the unpalatalized proto-Romanian /s/. considered diachronically, the pronunciation of the primitive unpalatalized /s/ + /i/ and the preservation of the proto-Romanian /ny/, found on the same territory with archaic remnants, appear as a natural continuation of the two identical phenomena from proto-Romanian. It cannot be maintained that the pronunciation of /n/ would have appeared in the dialect of the people in the Banat in a more recent period, which is also true for the pronunciation of unpalatalized /s/ + /i/. Both are cases of archaic phenomena preserved in local dialects. That which today, from a synchronic perspective, appears as a strange phonetical anomaly, in proto-Romanian constituted a phonetical norm. it is unquestionable that, beginning with the sixth and seventh centuries, the two pronunciations (with /s/ and with /ş/) coexisted for centuries, being in competition with each other, until the innovation with palatalized /ş/ was generalized in the greatest part of the Romanian linguistic territory (during the tenth and eleventh centuries). In some more conservative dialects, however, especially in those regions where the mark of Latinity had been imprinted more deeply on the phonetical physiognomy of the language, such as in Oltenia, the Banat, and southeastern Transylvania, the old proto-Romanian pronunciation with unpalatalized /s/ + /i/ was preserved. If the pronunciation with /ş/ represents today the victory of an innovation that appeared in the fifth and sixth centuries, the pronunciation with /s/ represents the last resistance, in local, isolated areas, of a phonetical archaic remnant of Latin origin. To the objection that the palatalization of /s/ + /i/ represents a "phonetical rule" in the evolution of the Romanian language, we answer that this is certainly incontestable, but it does not exclude the possibility that certain regional dialects preserved, in isolated areas, the proto-Romanian pronunciation with the palatalization /s/. The fact can also be observed in the case of the softening of the consonants /l'/ and /n/, transformed into /i/ in Dacian-Romanian. This did not prevent the dialect in the Banat from preserving, at a local level, the pronunciation *vine* (for *vie*)[13] and the dialect of the Changos from preserving the pronunciation with /l'/, *eu l'eu, tu l'ei, el l'e* (for *eu ieu, tu iei, el ie* = I take, you take, he takes).

4. Assuming that the depalatalization of /s/ has resulted from tendencies that appeared in the language as a result of foreign influence, as Mircea Borcilă suggested, then the influence had the paradoxical function of consolidating a tradition of pronunciation inherited from vulgar Latin.[14] We consider, however, the most logical hypothesis to be the most plausible, namely that the phenomenon that in all European languages descends from proto-Slavonic or proto-German must descend in Romanian from proto-Romanian, in other words it is a reflex from vulgar Latin.

5. Just like the old Fr. *toussir*, It. *tossir*, Eng. *tussir*, from all the Western Romance dialects that preserve the Latin pronunciation with unpalatalized /s/, in the same way the Romanian *tusâre* from the two dialects we mentioned represents a proto-Romanian pronunciation,

---

[13]I. Stan, "Observaţii asupra evoluţiei /ny/ < /i/ in the Romanian language," in *Cercetări de linguistică*, IV, 1959, p. 49.

[14]See a similar observation of Al. Graur, *Evoluţia limbii române*, Bucureşti, 1963, p. 76.

preserved on a regional level, of the same pronunciation from vulgar Latin (*tussire*).

The sibilant pronunciation appears therefore to be an archaic phonetical permanence, by which Daco-Romanian is related to the group of Western Romance languages, and one of the phonetical links between vulgar Latin and some of the regional Daco-Romanian dialects. The phonetical evolution of the Romanian language does not exclude the possibility of the preservation, in isolated dialectal areas, of the old Latin /s/, also preserved in other Romance languages.

Arguments like these were never brought to support the hypothesis of the Cuman or Hungarian origin of the sibilant pronunciation in the dialect of the Changos. The permanence of the archaic pronunciation with the unpalatalized Latin /s/ represents a valuable indication regarding the uninterrupted continuity north of the Danube of an old Romance population of sibilant dialect from the Roman period until today.

* * *

Generally, names are given to human collectivities because of a strange feature, an odd habit, or a defect that leaves a strong impression on other people. In the process of Szecklerization, the Changos pronounced a corrupted Hungarian, mixing Romanian sounds with Hungarian ones. Especially the sibilant Romanian pronunciation transposed into Hungarian irritated the Szecklers, who invented a name for those who spoke that way, calling them *Changos* (Hung. *csángók*). Later, this name became generally accepted.

Viewed from a modern perspective, the old sibilant pronunciation of some regional dialects appears strange, sometimes even ridiculous to Romanians as well. We should not, however, lose sight of the fact that, sixteen centuries ago, this was the common, traditional pronunciation on the entire territory of Dacia. Due to certain special conditions of historical evolution, some of the people in the Banat and the Changos preserved it for many centuries after it disappeared from the common language. Asked why they pronounce this way, the speakers do not know, they just shrug their shoulders: *Nu scim, asă-i la noi, asă o grăit bătrânii, asă am apucat...* ("We do not know, this is our way, this is how our ancestors spoke, this is how we learned...").

3. The Preservation of /l'/ (Palatalized)

Already in the primitive Romanian language, the consonant *l* followed by /é/ (short, stressed /e/) and by /í/ (long, stressed /i/) was palatalized, being pronounced /l'/, and later on, in the Daco-Romanian dialect, it was vocalized, being pronounced /i/, sometime in the sixteenth century.[15] The phenomenon included both Latin and the Slavic elements:

Lat.	linum	l'in	in (flax)
	leporum	l'epure	iepure (rabbit)
	levo	l'eu	ieu (I)
Old Sl.	ljutu	l'ute	iute (fast)
	krali		crai (king)

The /l'/ stage is still preserved in the dialects south of the Danube. In the Chango dialect it has partially been maintained until today, for centuries after its transformation in Dacian-Romanian, representing an example of belated evolution. According to the attestation of some older informants, at the time when they were children (at the end of the nineteenth century), the present indicative of the verb *a lua* (to take) was pronounced this was in the Catholic villages in the northern group: *l'eu, l'ei, l'e, luăm, luaţi, l'eu* (I take, you take, he takes, we

---

[15]Cf. Florica Dimitrescu, *op.cit.*, p. 96.

take, you take, they take). This old pronunciation can still be heard in the dialect of some old people in Bartice\u015fti, Gher\u0103e\u015fti, Pilde\u015fti, Corhana, Adjudeni (in the county of Neam\u0163), and H\u0103l\u0103uce\u015fti (in the county of Ia\u015fi).[16]

In S\u0103b\u0103oani I heard pronunciations like these: *l'e gi be, nu ci-ngie* (for *ia de bea, nu te-mbia* = go ahead and drink), *l'e musca gin lapci* (for *ia musca din lapte* = take the fly out of the milk), *l'e sama, m\u0103i b\u0103ieci* (for *ia seama, m\u0103i b\u0103iete* = be careful, boy), *l'e m\u00e2na gi pi mini* (for *ia m\u00e2na de pe mine* = take your hand off me). The imperative form *l'e* was transferred to the local Hungarian dialect. In S\u0103b\u0103oani and Pilde\u015fti they still say *l'e te* (take), which proves that this pronunciation was so frequent in the past that it was transmitted to the Hungarian dialect as well. Such old Romanian pronunciations, in the dialect of a population usually considered to be of Hungarian origin, are not fortuitous and are not borrowed from the Moldavians either. They are inherited from the old Transylvanian Romanian dialect that the Changos were speaking before their linguistic Szecklerization, in a period when the pronunciation with /l'/ (palatalized) still existed in Daco-Romanian (in the fifteenth and sixteenth centuries). At that time their ancestors spoke only Romanian. Regarding the bilingualism that appeared later and has been partially preserved until today in S\u0103b\u0103oani, we mention the fact noted by Gustav Weigand and reported by the Hungarian linguist Rubinyi M\u00f3zes, that the Changos cannot even pronounce certain sounds of the Hungarian language, which they speak like children when they learn the sounds of the language. On the other hand, when they speak Romanian, they still use medieval pronunciations. We believe that the only conclusion that can be drawn

---

[16]Wanting to pick up the ball of a little girl, Maria Copila\u015f, from Bartice\u015fti, she answered energetically: "*Las\u0103 c-o l'eu ieu*" ("I'll take it"), in which the pronunciation *l'eu* could be heard very clearly. It was not a childish pronunciation, because her mother and grandmother pronounced the same way.

from this is that the so-called Changos are Romanians, who were Szecklerized (more or less) in the past in Transylvania.[17]

---

[17]Suggestive for the bilingualism of a minority of them is the incident related to Iosif Petru M. Pal in his book *Originea catolicilor din Moldova şi franciscanii, păstorii lor de veacuri.* In the summer of 1936, Onisifor Ghibu, professor at the university of Cluj, visited Săbăoani, where he talked with the inhabitants, whom he asked:

"What are you?"

"Romanians!" they answered.

"What do you mean Romanians? Do you not speak Hungarian?"

"Well, sir," a young man answered, "this language is a misfortune for us!" (p. 73).

The historical misfortune that the young man in Săbăoani was talking about was the process of Szecklerization the victims of which were most of the Romanians in the Szeckler region, among whom were the predecessors of the Changos. The people have preserved the tradition that they are Romanians, but the "misfortune" of the Hungarian language makes it hard for the others to believe that; moreover, some authors see in this "misfortune" the proof of their Hungarian origin. Certainly this dialect proves something, namely the linguistic Szecklerization of the Transylvanian Romanians, and not their Magyar origin.

Chapter 17

A Description of the Dialect: Vocabulary

1. Religious Terminology

There are many observers who admit that the Chango phenomenon involves so many Romanian structural elements that it is very difficult to differentiate the Changos from the Moldavian Romanians. A nineteenth century Hungarian historian, Elek Gekö, who visited them in 1838, found so many non-Hungarian elements about them, in their language, costume, customs, and way of life, that he drew the correct conclusion that the Changos are not of Hungarian origin.[1]

What confuses many Romanian observers today, especially those who are not familiar with the process of Szecklerization, is their belonging to the Catholic religion. If the Changos were not Catholics, no one would be tempted to consider them of Hungarian origin. There are even some communities whose inhabitants, after their settling in Moldavia, became converted to the Orthodox religion. This is the case of the villages Budeşti and Bălţăteşti (in the county of Neamţ), where the inhabitants knew and used for a long time the sibilant

---

[1](Editor's Note) Many authors claim the non-Magyar origin of the Changos, but, at the same time, they claim them for the Magyar nation.

Transylvanian dialect,[2] and today are considered Moldavians, being Orthodox and speaking the Moldavian dialect. But their relatives who remained Catholic are considered of Hungarian origin. Consequently, the religious criterion is not valid for establishing ethnic belonging. What happened to the Catholic Istro-Romanians, who lived alongside the Croatians, also happened with the Szecklerized Catholic Romanians in Transylvania, as a consequence of their symbiosis with the Szecklers. Due to historical conditions, many Romanians became converted to the Catholic religion. This fact is interpreted and presented as proof of their Hungarian origin. They, however, consider themselves to be of Romanian nationality and language. But the old confusion between religion and national belonging is still maintained and therefore people consider them as such. What we discover under the surface, however, does not support this opinion. We find that the entire religious substratum inherent to their way of thinking and life is Romanian, and the religious terminology with its archaic and folkloric character is entirely of Latin Slavic origin. Even a series of notions specific to Western Catholicism have Slavic names. Thus, in the Chango Romanian dialect, the bishop is called *vlăgicî* (*vlădicî*), the Mass is *sluzbî* (*slujbî*), the short evening ceremony is *visernî* (*vecernie*), the rosary is called *mătanii*,[3] the prayers are *osinasî* (*ocinaşî*), the sermon is called, in some villages, *căzanii*, the burial service is *prohod*, and the priest *sluzăsci, spovegesci, împărtăsăcsi, bocadi, cununî*, etc. Other terms are: *Maica Domnului, Maica Presista, Sfânta Fisoarî, nir, iertăsune,*[4] *groapî, gropniseri, pomanî,*

---

[2]Domokos Pál Péter, *op. cit.,* p. 97.

[3](Editor's Note) For example, the phrase *a înconjura mătăniile* (*a recita rozariul* = to recite the rosary).

[4](Editor's Note) In the past, the Catholic church singers in Moldavia were "pardoned" at funerals. This Transylvanian custom was banned by the church superiors, together with other practices at funerals which were considered pagan. The "pardoning" of the

pominiri, comând,[5] bosit, Crăsun, Bobosadî, Stracenii, Florii, Pasci, Ispas, Rusalii, Sânketru, Sândâieni, Sâncilii, Sântî-Mării, înzer,[6] dracu, nicuratu, spurcatu, usigă-l crusa sî tămâia, Doamni-azutî, Doamni firesci sî aparî, bodaprosci,[7] etc.

The massive presence of the traditional Orthodox terminology in the dialect of the Catholic Changos, presumed Hungarians, who have lived for centuries in the discipline of the western church and under the severe authority of the Latin clergy, causes bewilderment. What is the explanation of this terminology and Romanian traditions in their language and mentality? At the same time, how can we interpret the

---

dead was removed with difficulty, as revealed by the very harsh order given by Bishop Camilli, on the occasion of his official visit to Răchiteni (12-14 July 1912): "Pardoning is forbidden both in and outside the church; if a church singer disobeys this ordinance, he will be suspended: first for a period of three months, then for six months, and third forever" (*Arhiva Episcopiei Catolice din Iaşi*, dosar XIII, vol. 12, f. 42). Cf. the ordinance no. 9: "We advise and persistently urge that everybody try hard to uproot the heathen customs amidst the Christian people, customs which are still practices, especially at funerals" (Nicolae Iosif, *Acte pastorale...*, I, Iaşi, 1913, pp. 72-73). "The pardoning" at weddings, of a different kind, is still practiced today.

[5](Editor's Note) In the manuscript left by Antonio Mauro (1797), a related Transylvanian term is attested to: *comândare*, "funeral feast in the memory of the dead," in which not only the church singer, but also the priest took part, as it happens today (see Carlo Taglivini *op. cit.*, p. 100); over time, *comândare* was replaced with *praznie*.

[6](Editor's Note) There is also the christening name *Inger*, with the diminutive *Ingerel* (the phonetism *inger, ingerel* is frequent in certain regions in Transylvania; Sextil Puşcariu explains the transformation of initial *în- (îm-)* into *in- (im-)*, as "the second base of the influence exerted by the soft position upon the preceding vowel, in the pre-Romanian epoch, a phenomenon which, however, was not generalized or which did not become collective" (see "Pe marginea cărţilor," in *Dacoromania*, V, 1927-1928, p. 779). See also *Anghel* (not used by the Catholics in Moldavia) and the It. *Angelo*, which, in our opinion, was given by the Italian missionaries

[7](Editor's Note) The Hungarian translation *istanfidăsa* (<*Isten fizesse*, "May God reward") was later superposed on this Slavic thanksgiving formula (according to Dumitru Mărtinaş' notes).

total absence of the Hungarian terminology and specific character? Could there be a more obvious proof of their Romanian ethnic-linguistic base and a more striking confirmation of Nicolae Iorga's intuition, who says about them that they are not by far the foreigners one might believe them to be? History and language offer us the only possibility to understand the so-called Chango enigma. Becoming converted to Catholicism, their predecessors changed only the external form of their religion, passed under a different ecclesiastical authority, but did not change their spiritual base and their old mentality, did not renounce their customs, and maintained their traditional religious terminology.

We are not denying the fact that, due to the Roman canonical discipline, their spiritual base did not acquire more vigor, with positive consequences in public and family life, but its innermost structure remained unchanged. Returning to terms, in Transylvania, the homiliary (*cazania*) was for a long time the fundamental sermon book, and that is why in some Catholic villages the sermon is still called *căzănie* (homily), and the priest *căzănuiesci*, preaches homilies in church. The text of the prayers may have undergone many changes, but the common people still call them *osinasî*, as they were called in the sixteenth century. The Mass was celebrated, until recently, in the Latin language, but its name remained Slavic – *sluzbî*. The traditional Easter eggs decorated with painted crosses are still called *ouă încrscici,* from the old Slavic *kristu* (cross), and so on. These are traditions inherited from the old times and they further demonstrate that the theory about the Hungarian origin of the Changos, based on the criterion of their religious belonging, is invalid, as their religious terminology and the linguistic and folkloric evidence demonstrates. The language and folklore are clear, unlike some tendentious theses of the historians who are often influenced by other interests than scholarly truth. The Megleno-Romanians became Mohammedans, the

Istro-Romanians are Catholics, but no one has ever maintained that because of this they would not be Romanians. Only in the case of the Changos the perspective is different. Being Catholics, they are considered to be of Hungarian origin, although even today they speak a very old Romanian dialect. But nothing could make them forget that they are Romanians.

2. Family Names

In the church registers of the Catholic parishes in Moldavia we notice an interesting situation. Let us analyze, for example, the case of a village in the county of Bacău, Luizi-Călugăra, where the Transylvanian inhabitants settled between the years 1730-1740. In addition to a percentage of Hungarian names, approximately 30%, out of which many are Romanian names translated into Hungarian, the majority of the names are Romanian: *Bârsan, Mocanu, Giurgiu, Lupan, Zaharia, Solomon, Gălăţanu, Moraru, Păuleţ, Tulbure, Colţa, Fânaru, Cazacu, Iancu, Butacu, Butăcel, Armanu, Lupu,*[8] *Cojocaru, Olaru, Voinea, Macarie, Marcu, Condac, Cernica, Jitaru, Clopotaru, Bogdan, Bogdănel, Bălan, Sumănaru, Mititelu, Pătraşcu, Vornicu,*[9] etc. Similar situations are found in the registers of other villages as well.[10] Romanian family names prevail everywhere, in a proportion of

---

[8]An offspring of this family, Andrei Lupu, was the first hero who fell in Bulgaria during the War for Independence (in the night of 13/14 August 1877).

[9]Iosif Petru M. Pal, *op. cit.,* p. 52.

[10]Even in Găiceana (in the county of Bacău), where today the inhabitants consider themselves Hungarians, an indication that the process of Szecklerization affected the deeply and entailed a change of consciousness, in addition to many Hungarian names, there are enough Romanian names as well: *Avădanei, Baciu, Ciobanu, Cojocaru, Spătaru, Rotaru, Blăjuţ, Cojan, Cernica, Bogdan, Juratu, Guşa, Iancu, Petrici, etc.* (see Petru Râmneanţu, *Problema iradierii românilor din Transilvania în principatele române,* p. 143).

about two-thirds. Judging by their Romanian costume, the inhabitants of Luizi-Călugăra can be nothing else but Romanians. They consider themselves Romanians. Unfortunately, the Romanian administrative authorities in the past considered that all the inhabitants of this village, as well as those in other Catholic villages in Moldavia, were Hungarians, because of their religion, helping to substantiate, in this way, incorrect theories about their origins.

The onomastics of the Changos in Moldavia is very similar to that of the Romanians in Transylvania, because it took shape in the same historical conditions. Regardless of the family names they have and of how they are looked upon by others, they know that they are Romanians and live according to their old Romanian customs.

(Editor's Note) At Tămăşeni (in the county of Neamţ) – one of the oldest Catholic villages in Moldavia, deserted at the end of the seventeenth century (in 1682, Vito Piluzio remarked that *homini nono sono* here) and repopulated after 1744 – among the family names from the period 1804-1919, we find names as the following: *Pîrţac, Căliman, Cimpoieş, Ştef, Andrieş, Scripcar, Petrişor, Petre,* Constantin, *Olaru, Antoci, Antohi, Burcă, Dabija, Leahu, Busuioc, Puţan, Buzău, Munteanu, Moraru, Cozma, Gherguţ, Prăjescu, Vătămănel, Antonică, Pascaru, Petruţ,* etc. (Iosif Gabor, *Tămăşeni. File din trecut,* pp. 103-107).

At Gherăieşti, 27 of 40 Romanian family names are registered in the parish rolls of 1800. At Fărăoani (in the county of Bacău), C. Lozincă indicates the following names: Pătraşcu, Novac, Matei, Panţiru, Buteanu, Cojocaru, Pescaru, Bejan, Vaida, Corbu, Roşaţă, Bălan, Jitaru, Cobzaru, Ciurariu, Demşa, Plop, Maior, Munteanu (see Revista istorică, XXI, 1935, p. 403). The author had received a letter from N. Iorga (August 1931), in which the Romanian scholarly historian pointed out that: "the Romanian names are decisive" (see "Românii din satele catolice," in Poporul românesc, V, 1935, p. 52). Most of the families in Săbăoani are named Cobzaru, Ciobanu, and Robu.

3. Regionalisms of Latin Origin

a. Ler (Lat. *lever* = brother-in-law)

A valuable lexical inheritance, descending from vulgar Latin and which has disappeared from contemporary Romanian,[11] is their term of kinship *ler, leru-neu* (brother-in-law, my brother-in-law), with the vocative *lerule,* and the diminutive *lerisorule,* with the meaning of brother-in-law. The term has no connection with the meaning or origin of the word *ler* from the refrains of carols and has only been preserved in the dialect of the Changos, being frequent especially in the northern group. It probably circulated in other regional dialects as well, from which it disappeared without a trace, competing with and then being eliminated by its synonym *cumnat* (<Lat. *cognatus*). According to oral testimony, which we could not verify personally, *ler* is also heard here and there in the language of the old people in some of the villages at the foot of the Codru Mountains (Archiş, Beliu, Groşeni, Nermis, and Răpsog, in the county of Arad). The dictionaries of the Romanian language and regional glossaries do not register it, an indication that the term disappeared a long time ago. Vasile Scurtu, the erudite scholar of Romanian kinship terms does not know it either.[12] It appears that it circulated in the past in Daco-Romanian, possible proof being the toponym *Lereşti* and the family names *Lerescu, Lereanu,* which imply the root *ler.* This term of kinship represents a vestige of Latin origin, because both semantically, as well as according to the norms of the historical phonology of the Romanian language, it derives from the Latin *lever,* which later became *lévir, léviri* (with long, stressed */é/*), that appears in all lexicons of the Latin language

---

[11]See also *supra,* pp. 64-65.

[12]Vasile Scurtu, *Termenii de înrudire în limba română,* Bucureşti, 1966.

with the meaning of brother-in-law. The fall of /v/ in intervocalic position gave birth to the Romanian *ler.* According to Quicherat,[13] the Latin *levir* is found with the same meaning in the works of the Latin writers Festus and Isodorus (during the sixth and seventh centuries), as well as in emperor Justinian's *Digeste,* where it is used as juridical term, with the clear specification of its meaning: *vir sororis levir est,* exactly the same as in the dialect of the Changos, in which the husband of an older sister is called *ler,* implying a connotation of respect when it is used by younger brothers-in-law. It is interesting that this popular and juridical Latin term from the sixth century, which has disappeared from all the Romanian dialects (except, perhaps, the above mentioned villages from the county of Arad), has been preserved in the regional Chango dialect, with an identical semantic content and with almost the same sonorous framework as in Latin. For the Romanian language, this dialect has the merit of having circulated a unique Latin term and the phenomenon of sibilant pronunciation from vulgar Latin until today. The word *ler* being unknown to the Romance idioms and languages of neighboring peoples, it results that it could only be preserved and transmitted by a Daco-Roman population, that spoke *ab initio* in a Romance language, ever since the distant times of their origins. The circumstances that led to the disappearance of this word on the entire romance territory of Romania and to its preservation only in the small area of the Chango dialect is difficult to elucidate.

It was preserved in Transylvanian Daco-Romanian, but later disappeared from it, being only maintained in an isolated area of this dialect. Just like in the case of the sibilant pronunciation, this illustrates once again the archaic and conservative character of the

---

[13]L. Quicherat and A. Davelny, *Dictionaire latin-francais,* ed. XLIV, Paris, f.a., from where we took the information and the quotation.

respective dialect, confirming Bartoli's theory of the conservatism of isolated lateral area[14]

The preservation of this term only or almost only in the Chango dialect, and its circulation throughout the course of the entire history of the Romanian language disproves the theory that the Changos form *a moldvai magyarság,* because in this case we would be dealing with an archaic term and an archaic phonetical phenomenon that descended on a direct line from vulgar Latin through the channel of some presumed Hungarians from Atelkuz or from the region of Raba of western Hungary, through the channel of some Hungarians who appeared in Pannonia only at the end of the ninth century, a hypothesis which, evidently, is not plausible. It results that these heirs and bearers of such Latin elements can only be a branch of Transylvanian Daco-Romanians.

But the word *ler* implies another interesting aspect. It was transferred with the same meaning in the Hungarian Chango dialect as well, under the form *ler-em* and *ler-eszkem* (Rom. *lerule, lerişorule*). The same happened with the terms *a corinda* (to carol) and *păcurar* (shepherd), which entered the Hungarian Chango dialect under the form *korindálni* and *pakurár*.

The supporters of the theory that the Changos are of Hungarian origin must solve this thorny problem: were these three terms of Latin origin transferred from Romanian into Hungarian or from Hungarian into Romanian? The answer is too obvious: they were transferred from Romanian into Hungarian, because the Hungarian language had no way of inheriting them from the Latin language. In Hungarian they were introduced by the Changos, who, during the process of Szecklerization, besides a series of specific phenomenon, transposed in their adopted dialect a significant number of Romanian lexical

---

[14]See Sextil Puşcariu, *Limba romảna.* I. *Privire generală,* Bucureşti, p. 212.

terms, among them some pastoral and kinship terms. These Romanian terms transposed by them in Hungarian illustrate both the Romanian origin of the Szecklerized Changos, as well as the priority in time of their Romanian dialect over their later bilingualism. In other words, *before they spoke Hungarian, the Changos spoke Romanian.* The same priority, historically, of the Romanian dialect over the Hungarian one is proven by the sibilant pronunciation, the affrication of the dentals, the yodization of /e/, the pronunciation with /s/, of the Hungarian affricate /cs/, the transfer of the Romanian vowel /ă/, phenomena that we find in the respective dialect in the village of Săbăoani. It is interesting to note that, while the Hungarian Chango dialect is full of Romanian phonetical phenomena, the Romanian dialect of the Changos does not know any phonetical phenomena that could be attributed to Hungarian influence. The fact is explained historically: the Romanian dialect of the ancestors of the Changos was spoken centuries before the coming of the Hungarians and the Szecklers to Transylvania.

Consequently, one cannot speak about the Changos as Hungarians. They represent an old Transylvanian Romanian population, and the fact that in the past they underwent a transient process of Szecklerization, which was, for the most part, erased, does not justify claims that the Changos are Hungarians.

b. Corindă (<Lat. kalenda)

In Romanian folklore the term *colindă* (carol, with *l*), of Latin origin, through Slavic channels (Lat. *kalenda* > old Sl. *kolenda* > Rom. *colindă*), is well-known.[15] Like some Transylvanian dialects, the Chango Romanian dialect also knows the variant *corindă* (with *r*),

---

[15](Editor's Note) See *NALR pe regiuni. Transilvanian,* issue no. 630 (manuscript).

inherited directly from Latin: *kalenda > cărindă > corindă*, which had an extended area of circulation, together with the derivatives: *a corinda* (to carol), *corindat* (caroling), *corindător* (caroler).

> *Noi sâncem **corindători**,*
>
> *Nu stăm noapca pi cupciori.*
>
> *Am vinit la **corindat**,*
>
> *La hăit sî la urat,*
>
> *La gospodari gin sat...*

Lately the word *corindă* has begun to disappear in many villages. In some of them it has already disappeared, under the influence of school and of the Moldavian dialect. It can still be heard in the speech of some old women in certain isolated villages. The term is part of the old lexical Transylvanian base of the Romanian Chango dialect and proves that the territorial origin of this dialect is Transylvanian. It also confirms the ties that existed in an older period between the ancestors of the Changos and other Transylvanian dialects. As we have seen, the derivative *a corinda* was transposed in the Hungarian Chango dialect under the form of *korindalni*.

c. The Romanian *soţ* (husband)

The fact, also attested in other regions, that the women frequently call their husbands with the appellative *român* (Romanian): *măi române, românu-neu, n-o vinit românu, n-o murit românu,* is very significant. If they had a consciousness that they are Hungarian, they would certainly not call their husbands by this name.[16]

---

[16](Editor's Note) This fact was initially recorded by P. (Bonaventura) Morariu, "Istoricul satului şi parohiei Hălăceşti," in *Almanahul... "Viaţa,"* 1925, p. 64. As far as its attestation in other regions is concerned, see *ALR* II, h. 129, and *ALRM* II/I, h. 211.

Conclusions

Language is the most precious treasure that children inherit from their parents... It is the emblem of nobility, the testimony of the nationality of a people.

– Vasile Alecsandri

1. Peoples are one and the same with the traditional language that they inherited from their ancestors. The origin and the past of peoples are mirrored in their native langue, which makes them whole and defines their existence.

Depending on the historical circumstances in which it lives, a population may sometimes be compelled to adopt the language of another population with which it coexists. This is how bilingualism is born. This is what happened to the Changos, who, living for a long time together with the Szecklers, acquired the Hungarian language of the latter. In a case like this, the historian must differentiate between the two elements of this bilingualism: the primary element, which is the primitive linguistic stratum inherited from their predecessors, and the secondary element, which is the linguistic substratum adopted under the pressure of historical events. The state of bilingualism is usually also altered due to such events, either by forgetting or by permanently adopting the secondary language. In this case, the bilingual Transylvanian Changos who settled in Moldavia in the thirteenth century quickly abandoned the Hungarian language, the secondary element of their bilingualism, which they forgot completely, continuing to speak Romanian in their sibilant dialect brought from Transylvania, becoming monolingual again, like in their pre-Hungarian historical period.

2. For the Changos in Moldavia, their Transylvanian Romanian dialect represents their most valuable cultural inheritance, preserved from their Romanian predecessors in Transylvania. The studying of this linguistic and historical document offers us today the main source of information and documentation on their historical past, their origin, and their whole historical-linguistic evolution. Without studying this dialect, their historical past cannot be understood.

3. All the Italian missionaries from the eighteenth and nineteenth centuries confirmed the existence of the Romanian dialect of the Changos. Even Petru Zöld, a Szeckler missionary, attested that they all spoke Romanian. Only the ecclesiastical authorities in Transylvania and Hungary, tendentiously misinformed, were denying this to Rome, with the precise purpose of eliminating the Italian missionaries from Moldavia and replacing them with Hungarian ones. Fortunately, the pope and the Congregation for Fide Propaganda knew the reality very well and therefore refused to accede to this demand.

4. Finally, the Hungarian linguist Gábor Szarvas (1873), like other authors before him, observed that most of the Changos spoke Romanian. In his opinion, repeated by many authors up to the present-day, the Romanian dialect of the Changos was the result of their "Romanianization" by the Moldavians. Being insufficiently informed on the problems of Romanian dialectology, Szarvas confused their Transylvanian dialect with their Moldavian one, an inexcusable error from a scholarly point of view, and all the more serious for those who still maintain it today.

5. The most eloquent proof that this Romanian dialect existed in the past and has been spoken uninterruptedly is the fact that even

today the Changos, especially the old people, speak in their sibilant and affricating dialect, which, evidently, they could not have learned from the Moldavians who did not know it, but which they inherited from an older period, from their Romanian ancestors in Transylvania.

6. Just as in the past, in the time of the Transylvanian School, the study of the Romanian language illustrated and demonstrated the Latin origin and belonging of the Romanian language and people, in the same way, on a dialectal level, the study of the old Transylvanian dialect of the Changos illustrates and demonstrates the Transylvanian Romanian origin and belonging of its speakers. The key to the so-called enigma of the Changos is their own Romanian dialect, which they still speak today.

7. The old thesis of Hungarian historiography, viewed as an axiom in the science of the past, according to which the Changos would have been denationalized and linguistically assimilated by the Moldavian Romanians, did not take into consideration either their Romanian dialect or their Romanian origin, thus neglecting to explain the historical and linguistic evidence. Romanian-Hungarian bilingualism was a reality in the past for many Changos, but it was not due to their denationalization in Moldavia, but to their Szecklerization in Transylvania: the Romanians did not assimilate the Hungarian Changos, but the Magyar-Szecklers denationalized, in Transylvania, part of the Romanians. For the Changos, Moldavia was the refuge where they save their Romanian ethnic being.

8. The present dialectal dualism of the Changos in Moldavia has a precise historical significance, namely that before acquiring the Moldavian dialect, they spoke Romanian in their own Transylvanian dialect. Therefore, they could not have been Romanianized by the Moldavians when they were already Romanians. The Moldavians did not lend them a new language, did not impose a new linguistic consciousness on them, they did nothing other than influence them

indirectly, through inherent everyday contact, to acquire the Moldavian dialect as well.

9. The fact that the Hungarian dialect was forgotten by the great majority of the Changos was not the effect of any supposed Romanianization. In the conditions of their escaping from Hungarian domination, the abandoning of the Hungarian dialect was the result of the reaction of their original Romanian ethno-linguistic base, that *reazione etnologica* that Ascoli talks about.[1] No longer needing the Hungarian language in their socio-economic and cultural relations, they abandoned this language imposed on them in the past in the Szeckler region, eventually forgetting it completely. The process of de-Szecklerization happened spontaneously, as a reflex the new historical conditions in Moldavia.

10. The sibilant dialect of the Changos represented for centuries the language of the family, of home (*die Heimsprache*), having the role of defender and preserver of their permanently threatened ethnic-linguistic individuality. The tenacity with which this dialect has been preserved, in extremely difficult conditions, against all forms of oppression, is reflective of the common struggle of the entire Romanian people for the preservation of their language and ethnic identity throughout the course of history, a fact which determined the humanist Bonifinius to say that the Romanians fought more for the preservation of their language than for their life. In our days, the same old dialect represents, from a scholarly standpoint, indisputable historical proof and concrete linguistic evidence of their Romanian origin and belonging.

11. The attempts made in the past to separate the Changos from the community of the Romanian nation encountered the invincible

---

[1]See Bogdan Petriceicu Hasdeu, *Etymologicum Magnum Romaniae,* I. Bucureşti, 1972, p. 26.

obstacle of the language, which proved once more that in the struggle for its existence and for the preservation of its national being, a people can maintain its identity as long as it does not abandon its language, the most dynamic force of national consciousness. The Changos have not forgotten their origin and have not abandoned their Romanian dialect.

12. To deny the Romanian origin of this population means not only to ignore a painful chapter in the Romanian historical past, but also to deny the linguistic evidence. The linguistic and historical reality of their Transylvanian Romanian dialect forms the fundamental basis for the study of this problem in the future.

13. The old popular tradition of the Changos regarding their Romanian origin is confirmed by the linguistic evidence. Given the Transylvanian Romanian dialect spoken by its great majority, this population in Moldavia cannot be viewed as an ethnic enclave of allogenous origin any longer, or as a cohabiting ethnic minority, but as a Romanian population of Transylvanian origin, as it has always been. Because the language is a living and defining inheritance for those who speak it, it does not and cannot deceive. It reflects objectively the truth of life and history.

14. The abandoning of the Hungarian dialect, a result of the Szecklerization process in the past, was determined by the reaction of the ethno-linguistic base and by the option of the population.

The present study represents a starting point for future scholarly inquiry into the origins and history of the Changos.

Appendix

Romanian Phonetical Elements in the Hungarian Chango Dialect

From a morphological and lexical point of view, the Hungarian Chango dialect is quite well-known today, due to both older and more recent research, the latter having been carried out assiduously by Hungarian linguists in Cluj, their results being gathered in the two volumes published by Gyula Márton.[1] The situation of the studying of this dialect from a phonetical standpoint is different. In our opinion, the results that have been obtained so far need some clarification.

From Gábor Szarvas on, all the Hungarian scholars have exclusively studied the Hungarian dialect spoken by a minority of Changos. They have all avoided and completely ignored the Romanian dialect spoken by their majority. One notices the same thing in the works by Gyula Márton, which are very valuable from the point of view of the Hungarian dialect, with one lacuna: they ignore the Romanian Chango dialect, as if it did not exist. But it does exist, is used today, and has exerted a strong influence on the Hungarian Chango dialect.

---

[1]Márton Gyula, *A moldvai csángó nyelvjárás roman kölcsönszavai; idem, Igetövek, igei jelek és személyaragk a moldvai csángó nyelvjárásban* (*Verbal Themes, Verbal Suffixes, and Personal Endings in the Chango Dialect in Moldavia*), Bucureşti, 1974.

Consequently, the phonetical system of this dialect, with a strange physiognomy, is a non-Magyar system, with a specific Chango (Romanian) character alien to the Magyar phonetical tradition. Knowing the phonetical system of the Romanian Chango dialect helps us unravel the enigma of the Hungarian dialect spoken by the Changos. In the process of linguistic Szecklerization, the Transylvanian Romanians could not get accustomed to the Finno-Ugric phonetical system of the Szeckler dialect, and, therefore, they transferred in the adopted dialect a great part of the phonetical system of their Romanian dialect, in this way giving birth to a new Hungarian dialect, the Chango Hungarian dialect, specific to the Szecklerized Romanians.

When, due to certain historical conditions, people have to learn a foreign language, in other words, when they pass from a traditional system of articulation of sounds to a new system of pronunciation characteristic of a different idiom, they cannot abandon their initial way of pronunciation, specific to their old base of articulation. Even when they manage to acquire the vocabulary and morphology of the new language, they cannot easily adapt themselves to the new way of articulating sounds, which they continue to pronounce according to the characteristics of their own native language. They bring into the new language certain predilections of pronunciation, a certain manner of intonation, of stressing, of rhythm, of speech, namely the imprint of the phonetical system of their original language. This is what the Dacians did when they learned the Latin language of the Roman colonists, what the assimilated Slavs did, who transmitted to the adopted Romanian language some ways of pronunciation characteristic to their language, what the Szecklerized Romanians did when they adopted the Hungarian language. Being a matter of the interference of two heterogeneous languages, the influence of the Romanian language on the morphological system of the Hungarian dialect is weak. This influence is very strong, however, on the phonetical system, because the Romanians, speakers of a Romance language, could not easily assimilate the vowel and consonantal system of Finno-Ugric type of the Hungarian language. Romanians cannot pronounce the Hungarian vowels /a/, /é/, /ö/, /ó/, /ü/, /ú/, which they replace with the closest Romanian vowels.

A Szeckler (Hungarian) word like *füstös* (smoked) is pronounced by the Changos *fisztësz* (*fistăs*), in which the Szeckler sibilant /s/ (Rom. /ş/) is replaced with the sibilant /s/, the vowels /u/ and /o/ are delabialized and pronounced in Romanian as /i/ and /ă/, because the Changos cannot pronounce the characteristic Hungarian sounds.

A Szeckler word like *az Isten* (God) is pronounced *z-Iszten* (*s-Istăn*), in which we notice four Romanian phonetical phenomena:

The apheresis of initial, unstressed /a/ in the article *az*, just like in the Romanian *miel* (lamb) from the Latin *agnellus;*

The agglutination of the article with the following word beginning with a vowel, forming a common unit with it in pronunciation (*z-Istăn*), which lends the article a specific Chango physiognomy;

The pronunciation of the Hungarian sibilant /s/ (Rom. /ş/) as /s/, because the Changos manifest an old intolerance toward the sibilants /ş/, /j/.

The replacement of the vowel /e/ with the Romanian vowel /ă/, unknown to Magyar vocalism.

In the Chango Hungarian dialect, especially the one in Săbăoani, the sonorous aspect of the word was submitted to a complete phonetical readjustment. The typical Hungarian sounds unknown to the phonetical system of the Changos, were replaced with similar sounds, borrowed from their old Romanian dialect. A characteristic of this dialect is especially the typical Chango-Romanian vocalism, with the prevalence of the Romanian vowels, especially the vowel /ă/ (ë), as well as the sibilant consonantism, reflexes of the phonetical system of the Chango Romanian dialect. Not knowing this Romanian dialect, the dialectologists in the past could not observe the close connection between the phonetical systems of the two dialects, the Romanian and the Hungarian, spoken by the Changos in the proportion that we have already shown.

The most characteristic Romanian interferences in the Hungarian dialect spoken in Săbăoani are the following:

The sibilant pronunciation /sz/, /z/ instead of /s/, /zs/ (Rom. /s/, /z/ instead of /ş/, /j/). For example: *pirosz* instead of *piros* (red), *Iozsi* (Iosif).

The affrication of the dentals /t/, /d/ + /e/, /i/, /y/, which are pronounced /cs/, /dzs/. For example: *z-ocsanok* instead of *az atyának* (father's), *kondzsei* instead of *kondei* (pen), *nédzs* instead of *négy, nedy* (four).

The pronunciation of the affricate /cs/ as /s/ (like Moldavian *socoi, soban*).[2] For example: *mosko,* instead of *macska* (cat), *sont,* instead of *csont* (bone), *sinálni* instead of *csinálni* (to do).

The pre-yodization of initial /e/, which becomes /ie/. For example: *iedësz* instead of *édes* (sweet), *ien* instead of *én* (I), *iedsz* instead of *egy* (one).

---

[2]In the polemic between Wichmann and Rubinyi (see the presentation of this polemic in László Mikecs, *op. cit.,* pp. 371-374), the Finnish linguist was right when he contradicted the legend according to which the Changos would pronounce the Hungarian affricate /cs/ as /c/, /s/, /sz/ (Rom. /ţ/, /ş/, /s/). Unlike the Hungarian authors, Wichmann had observed with accuracy that they pronounced this affricate with a softened /s/, intermediary between /s/ and /ş/, as in Moldavian *sutură, soc, somag.* Gustav Weigand had also noticed the same fricative sound in the dialect spoken in Visag, the Banat: *der Zwischenlaut zwischen /s/ und /s/* (see "Der rumanishen Dialekte de Kleinen Walachei, Serbiens und Bulgariens," in *Siebebter Jahresbericht...,* 1900, p. 50).

The massive penetration in the Hungarian vocalism of the Romanian vowel /ă/ (ë). For example: *z-embër* instead of *az ember* (the man), *ingëm* instead of *engem* (me), *esznëm* instead of *esnëm*.

All these are phenomena of Romanian-Chango type, identical with the same phenomena that we notice in the Romanian dialect of the Changos. They are not phenomena borrowed from the Moldavians, who do not employ the sibilant pronunciation and the affrication of the dentals. They are characteristic of their old sibilant Transylvanian dialect, from which they entered the Hungarian dialect during the process of Szecklerization, concomitantly with some Romanian terms (*lerem, lereszkem, korindálni, pakurár, pita,* etc.)[3] Such phonetical and lexical phenomena were transmitted conjointly into the adopted Hungarian dialect. It is not a matter of a belated, accidental influence, but of the inheritance of a phonetical system alien to the Hungarian language. It is a matter of the foreign pronunciation of some speakers who belonged to a different phonetical system, to a different base of articulation, and who could not assimilate the phonetics of the Hungarian language, which they substituted with their own phonetical system. This corrupted pronunciation of the Hungarian language, which is perceived as foreign, unpleasant to the linguistic consciousness of the Hungarians and the Szecklers, explains Petru Zöld's remark that the Changos speak Hungarian *multo blesius* (*sehr unangehehm*), as well as the nickname of *csángók,* created by the Szecklers.

The Hungarian dialect of the Changos on the valley of the Trotuş, of Szeckler origin, is phonetically different from the sibilant Hungarian dialect of the Changos of Romanian origin. The first one

---

[3](Editor's Note) "There are hundreds and hundreds of words of Romanian origin in the idiom of the Changos in Moldavia" (Gyula Márton, "Cîteva aspecte ale influenţei limbii române în lexical graiului ceangău din Moldova," in *Studii şi cercetări linguistice,* VI, 1955, nr. 3-4, iul.-dec., p. 332).

developed on a Szeckler substratum and dialectal base, and the second one developed on a Romanian substratum and linguistic base, still visible in the phonetical system of this dialect.

The non-Hungarian origin of the speakers of this sibilant Hungarian dialect was known in the past as well, but no one mentioned that they were or could be Romanian origin.

Index